PUFFIN BOOKS

# The SECRET LIVES of WOMEN SPIES

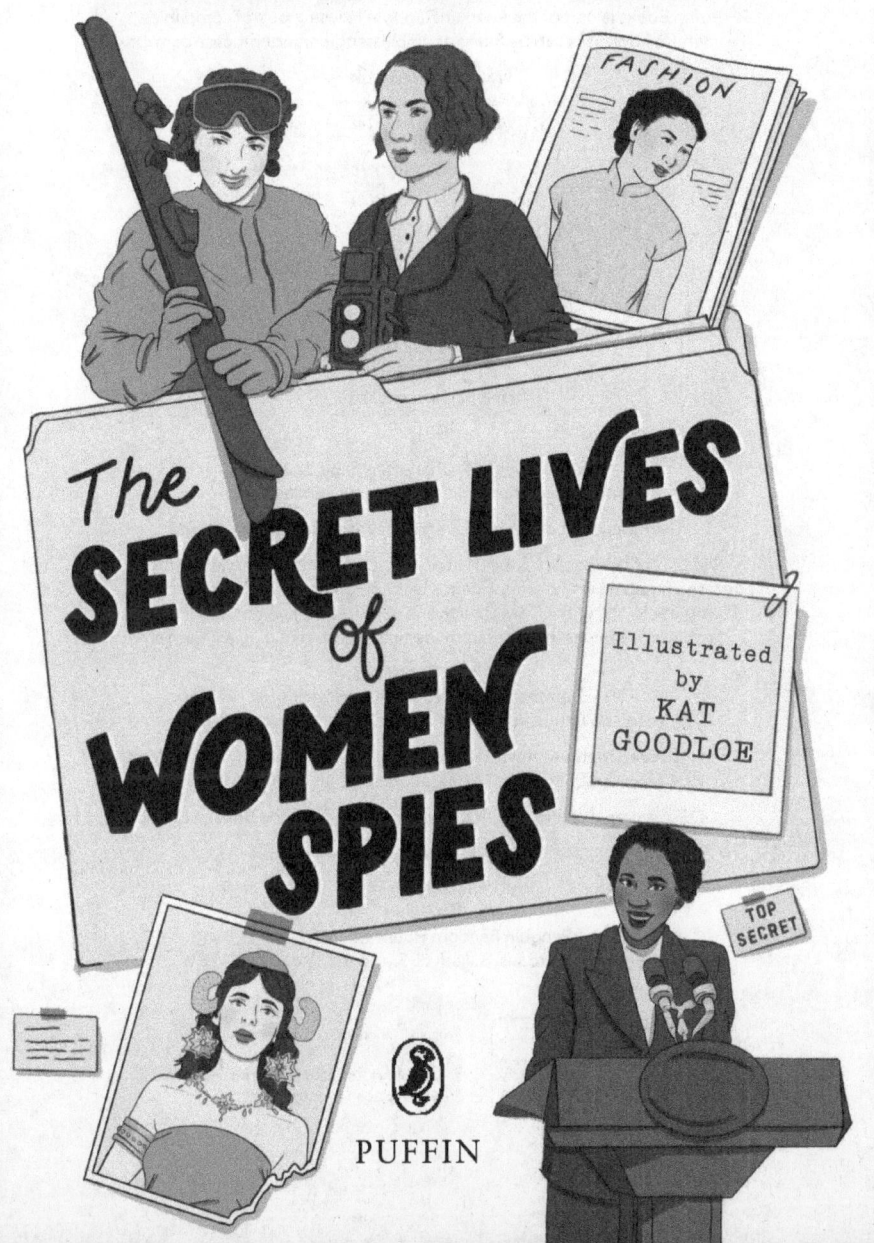

WRITER AND SPY-WATCHER

# CHARLOTTE PHILBY

FASHION

The
# SECRET LIVES
of
# WOMEN
SPIES

Illustrated
by
KAT
GOODLOE

TOP
SECRET

PUFFIN

PUFFIN BOOKS

UK | USA | Canada | Ireland | Australia
India | New Zealand | South Africa

Puffin Books is part of the Penguin Random House group of companies
whose addresses can be found at global.penguinrandomhouse.com

www.penguin.co.uk
www.puffin.co.uk
www.ladybird.co.uk

Penguin
Random House
UK

First published 2025

001

Text copyright © Charlotte Philby, 2025
Portrait illustrations copyright © Kat Goodloe, 2025

The moral right of the author and illustrator has been asserted

Set in 11/17pt Nietos
Typeset by Jouve (UK), Milton Keynes
Printed and bound in Great Britain by Clays Ltd, Elcograf S.p.A.

The authorized representative in the EEA is Penguin Random House Ireland,
Morrison Chambers, 32 Nassau Street, Dublin D02 YH68

A CIP catalogue record for this book is available from the British Library

ISBN: 978–0–241–70943–6

All correspondence to:
Puffin Books
Penguin Random House Children's
One Embassy Gardens, 8 Viaduct Gardens, London SW11 7BW

MIX
Paper | Supporting
responsible forestry
FSC® C018179

Penguin Random House is committed to a
sustainable future for our business, our readers
and our planet. This book is made from Forest
Stewardship Council® certified paper.

*For those women who hid in the shadows,*
*and deserve to stand in the light.*

# CONTENTS

Introduction    ix

Spy Speak    1
Spy Agencies    7
Elizebeth Smith Friedman    11
Edith Cavell    29
Harriet Tubman    47
Mata Hari    67
Josephine Baker    89
Famous Women You Didn't Know Were Spies!    108
Krystyna Skarbek    111
Noor Inayat Khan    128
Edith Tudor-Hart    147
Zheng Pingru    165
Saraswathi Rajamani    179
Zandra Flemister    192
Great Fictional Kid Spies    197

Glossary    201
Acknowledgements    209
About the Author    211

# INTRODUCTION

When I was a child (probably younger than you are now) I had two sets of grandparents. One set lived in Somerset, and on weekends my parents and I would jump in the car after school and drive three or so hours from London to see them. We'd eat peanut butter sandwiches and listen to story tapes on the way, our black and white Border collie, Bryn, whimpering on the back seat beside me.

It didn't seem particularly strange at the time, but going to visit my dad's father, Kim – or Grandpa Kimsky, as I knew him – was not so easy.

For one thing, we didn't know his address. Later in my life, my aunt drew me a map on the back of a napkin one lunchtime, to try to help me track down my grandfather's apartment in Moscow. By this time I was working as a newspaper journalist and planning to return to Russia for the first time as an adult, to learn about the man about who had become a mystery to me.

But we'll get to that.

What I did know back in the 1980s, as a kid with a heavy fringe and pink Converse boots, was that Kimsky and his wife lived in a city called Moscow, in Russia. If we wanted to write him a letter (which we did, regularly), we sent it from the letter box at the end of our road in London, addressed to a mailbox in the central post office in Moscow, on a street called Tverskaya.

Once a year, from when I was just three weeks old until Grandpa Kimsky's death when I was five and a half, my mum and dad and I flew to Russia to visit my grandfather and his wife, Rufina. Or as we knew her, Rufa.

I remember those moments clearly. Or maybe I'm remembering the photographs that exist from those days, kept behind plastic sheets in a thick leather album with gold trim. You know how that happens – sometimes you look at a photo you've seen many times before and you're not sure if it's the photo you're remembering, or the memory itself?

Rufa spoke little English and had bright red hair, which was cut just below her chin. She wore red lipstick and round glasses. Kim was older. On those family trips to Russia, he and my dad played chess for hours on the sofa in the living room with a pair of musket guns hanging on the wall behind them. As the men played, my mother drank tea and chatted with Rufa's family. I remember the constant swirl of cigarette smoke from the ashtray (I'm sad to say that my dad eventually died of lung cancer), and classical music booming from the record player. I remember snow falling on the school playground, which was visible through the window in my grandfather's study. I remember outings to a playground with carved wooden statues of bears.

But, on those family holidays, it was the journey from Sheremetyevo airport (the main airport in Moscow) to my grandfather's flat that has always stuck with me. As the plane touched down, my parents and I, unlike the other passengers, were met by men in grey suits, who led us away from the exit and ushered us into a car. From the back seat, they took out a blue light which they secured to the roof. The light was turned on, as was a siren, and we were driven down the motorway at full speed.

We were special guests.

Because Grandpa Kimsky was both my grandpa and the most infamous spy in history. He was two people at once.

On the one hand, Kim Philby was a loving father of five, who wore a white vest and braces while he played with me. On the other, he was a man who betrayed his country and his friends, and who was responsible for the deaths of countless people.

Born in India – where his father was working for the British government – Kim grew up in London, attending the famous Westminster School and then the University of Cambridge. His friends from this time remember him as charming and sometimes shy.

A handsome young man, Kim Philby was a typical upper-class Englishman – well-connected, with friends in high places. And this was precisely how he became a double agent.

While studying at Cambridge, Kim was one of a number of students who became interested in communism, and five of these students (including Kim) would go on to become a group of spies known as the 'Cambridge Five'.

Communism is a set of ideas for how the world should be run. It states that everyone should be equal and share things equally. In a communist country, or society, individual people do not own land or factories or machinery. Instead, the government who runs the society or country owns these things, and everyone is supposed to share them with everyone else, along with any money the government makes from it.

The problem is that often it doesn't work out like that. If you have a group of people telling everyone they have to be equal – or else! – it can create a system where some people are very powerful and have lots, and some people have nothing.

And if there are, right from the beginning, only a few people at the top of chain telling everyone else what to do, then the system is already broken. This is what happened in the Soviet Union during what became known as the Cold War (see page 159).

My family and I saw this when we visited Kim in Soviet Russia, the country that basically ran the Soviet Union, many years after Kim first learned about communism. There were queues of people around the block, waiting for the small amounts of food they were allowed to buy. Meanwhile, because we were guests of my grandfather – a person who was important to the government – we were given as much as we wanted, without having to wait in line.

So much for everyone sharing everything, equally.

Kim lived a very different life to this when, at the age of just 21 and having graduated from the University of Cambridge, he took off on his motorbike and headed to Austria. A professor at Cambridge had taught him about communism and how it could provide a better, more equal, world, and Kim liked the sound of it. So, with a little money in his pocket, he headed to Vienna, the capital of Austria, to help fight the Nazis and stop the rise of fascism through Europe.

Fascism is sort of supposed to be the opposite of communism. Where communism claims that everyone is equal, fascism says that some people are of less value than others, usually because of their race – and this was the ideology of Nazi Germany and its leader, Adolf Hitler. But actually there are strong similarities between the two systems. Both give the government strict control over their people, and the leaders who follow these ideas often rule through violence and fear.

The year that my grandfather travelled to Vienna, in 1933 (some years before the Second World War), fascism seemed to be everywhere. In Vienna, Kim secretly helped the communists fight against fascism. He spent time meeting with other communists and plotting a revolution to overthrow the fascist rulers. Posing as a tourist, he helped important communists, who were at risk of being arrested, travel through secret tunnels across the border to Czechoslovakia.

In top-secret meeting rooms across the city, he took apart weapons and smuggled their parts from one place to another on his motorbike. If he was stopped by the police, he would smile and show them his British passport and they would wave him on. They didn't believe a well-spoken Englishman could be part of the communist revolution.

It was in Vienna that summer when Kim became convinced he wanted to spend his life fighting for communism. And that the best way to do that would be to work for Soviet Russia, where communism had first properly been put into practice – even if it meant betraying Britain. The leaders of the NKVD (secret police whose role was to protect the Soviet Union) were desperate for someone like him. Someone who was English, who knew lots of people and who would never be suspected of working for another country. They couldn't have hoped for a better man for the job.

Kim was so good as a Soviet spy that in the years that followed, he managed to join the British

Secret Intelligence Service – the British spies – and climb his way up to become the head of its anti-Soviet section, which was the bit that was supposed to fight against communism. And while Kim was working for them, supposedly helping gain the upper hand against the Soviets, he was also working as a double agent, handing everything he discovered straight back to his Soviet bosses.

To some, Kim was a traitor, to others he was a hero.

The exact moment I learned the truth about my grandfather is hazy. But I do know that in the years that followed, I spent a lot of time reading about him. And the more I learned about him, the more questions opened up before me. Among them: *Where were all the women?*

In the many books and plays and films and true stories I found about the Cold War and the Cambridge Five, the stories all seemed to be about men.

There were a few female faces, but they were generally the secretaries or the wives or the girlfriends.

*Could it be true*, I wondered, *that the women were never really part of the action?* It didn't seem possible. Also, I knew that stories told from a certain point of view could overlook some of the important parts. Kim Philby, the legendary spy, had a wife and five children, for instance. He had also deceived them, and this seemed like a big deal to me.

But the family is rarely mentioned in any of the books or papers I have read about Kim Philby, the infamous double agent.

Women didn't just play small roles in Cold War history, of course. In fact, female spies have played some of the most important roles in espionage throughout the ages, as I will soon show you.

Why these women's amazing stories remain untold is harder to say. Perhaps it's because books about spying have mostly been written by men. Or maybe it's because female spies have rarely been caught? They're just that good.

One spy – a woman called Ursula Kuczynski, also known as Agent Sonya – was one day seen hanging out washing in her garden by the spy catchers (or 'rat-catchers' as they were sometimes known). *How could a mere housewife be any danger to us*, they thought. They just didn't believe she was a threat.

And this is part of the magic of women spies. The ability of the wife or mother or secretary to disappear into the background, unsuspected ...

Thankfully, recent historians like Shrabani Basu, Clare Mulley, Amy Butler Greenfield, Anne Sebba, Claire Hubbard-Hall and Dr Helen Fry are helping to shine a light on these largely unheard stories. I believe they teach us as much about how we think and talk about history, because of who gets to record it, as they do about the women themselves.

In my research about my grandfather, I learned about an extraordinary woman and secret agent so important to the Cold War that she was named by Anthony Blunt, one of the Cambridge Five, as 'the grandmother of us all'. I eventually wrote her story in my novel for adults *Edith and Kim*.

Edith Tudor-Hart was the woman who introduced and recruited Kim to the NKVD, so that he could go on to spy for the Soviets. She was never caught by the British. Until recently, her life was barely mentioned in the history books. If you have an interest in spying or in history – or indeed in anything! – you can visit the National Archives in London. There, among countless secret documents, is a mountain of files about Edith and her life, which were collected by the British secret service over the course of four decades. That's most of her adult life . . .

In 2015, as part of a project to release certain top-secret documents to the public, the files held on Edith Tudor-Hart were made available. My goodness, were there a few!

Edith was often accused by her friends and family of being paranoid when she said she was being watched by the British government. She was not being paranoid. The files the British secret service held on Edith go on for pages and pages and pages, and were collected over decades. There are notes about exactly what she did on the many days they followed her from her flat to her work. Or when she took her son, Tommy, who had a mental health condition, back and forth to the doctor for treatment.

British spies recorded her phone calls, and acted as moles, pretending to be Edith's friends or colleagues while feeding information about her back to the British government.

Edith first met my grandfather, Kim, during that summer of 1933. She moved to England the following year and then, throughout the Second World War, Edith passed on many secrets to the Soviet Union, often taking Tommy with her on her missions. Who would question why a young mother with a pushchair might be sitting alone on a park bench? Why would they bother lowering their voices to avoid sharing secrets in front of a woman nursing a baby in a station? She hid in plain sight.

Edith was also an amazing photographer, who used her camera as a tool for spying, photographing important and secret documents.

She even helped pass secrets to the Soviets about the development of the first atomic bomb. And all the while she was a devoted single mother.

Learning about Edith got me thinking about which other women spies might have been left out of history, and how incredible their tales might be. Because being a woman and a spy means being many people at once.

It turns out that there are more than a few examples of women secret agents at the centre of the action. Lots, in fact, and I couldn't possibly fit them all into a single book. So I have selected the ones whose story spoke to me, and those whose work helps bring to life the world in which they lived.

Brave, complicated, brilliant, terrible, inspiring, ruthless, passionate and tragic – the women whose lives I have written about in this book are nothing if not fascinating.

For each of them, I have included an introduction to our spy, followed by the story of their lives, looking back on what made them so remarkable. These read like the most extraordinary works of fiction, but they are all true. In order to write these stories, I have read and listened to various accounts of these women's lives – revealed in personal papers like letters and diaries, and in documents that governments once kept secret.

These women have led very different lives to me. So although what follows has all the historical facts correct, the emotions and feelings and smaller details have had to be imagined. But I hope, by attempting to bring them to life in this way, I can help us understand what it was like for these women to live in such extreme and often dangerous ways. To understand why they became spies, and the impact their choices had on themselves and those around them. And for some of the spies in this book, I instead thought the best way to tell their story was in imagined newspaper articles, which give an account of sometimes complicated lives, and decisions that sometimes had terrible consequences. You'll see these cropping up among the longer stories.

Ultimately, I hope this book helps shine a light on some of the lesser-known people in spying history. And in trying to understand the reasons why they were willing to risk their lives, and the lives of others, I hope it helps you understand a little more about the world we live in.

And remember, if you suspect a woman in your life of being a secret agent: Mum's the word.

# TOOLS OF HER TRADE

It is understandable that those involved in spying want to make their world as tricky to understand as possible. That's the whole point of being a spy – to be mysterious.

But sometimes the language we use to talk about the business of spying makes it almost impossible to get a sense of who is doing what to whom, and when. Let alone how. For that reason, I have included a glossary at the end of this book – a sort of mini dictionary which explains certain words and terms. Words that are included in the glossary will appear in bold (**like this**).

Once we've heard the extraordinary stories of each of our spies, we will also learn *the tools of her trade* – the tricks that our agents used to complete their work. These range from a talent for code-breaking to having friends in high places.

However, to give you a clear view into the murky world of espionage, we are going to start with a little masterclass of our own: our own spy toolbox. You might wish to refer back to this when you're reading later sections.

From explaining confusing spy speak, to outlining some important wars and events our secret agents were involved in, the section in the following pages will give you one of the most important tools of all: knowledge.

# SPY SPEAK

## ESPIONAGE

Espionage is the word used to describe the act of
spying or of using spies to find out information. Spies
are often hired by governments that run countries,
but not always. All sorts of industries and businesses
use spies. Companies might pay people to find out
secrets about, say, rival companies that they can use
to their advantage. As we will soon discover, spies
can belong to groups, or they can be lone rangers.
One thing is for sure: where there are secrets, there
are spies.

## INTELLIGENCE

Intelligence is secret information, and there
are usually two kinds. The first is political

intelligence – about another country's government. The second is military intelligence – gathered usually before or during a war about an enemy's possible use or development of weapons, or any planned attacks.

## INTELLIGENCE OFFICER

Working as an intelligence officer can mean many different things. But it will normally involve gathering secret information, and spending time trying to understand what the information means. If intelligence shows that there is a threat of some sort – normally to a country or company – it is the officer's job to pass this information on to the right people or organization, in order for the threat to be dealt with.

## AGENT

An agent is a person working for an intelligence service, often providing top-secret information. Agents aren't allowed to tell anyone what they do for a living.

## FIELD AGENT

A field agent is a person who secretly works as an agent in a particular country or area, where they have been carefully placed by their bosses.

## DOUBLE AGENT

A double agent is a spy who pretends to be working for one country, while secretly working for the country they are supposed to be spying against. Often, a double agent will produce disinformation to confuse or distract the organization that thinks the spy only works for them.

## DISINFORMATION

(Also known as *misinformation*.) This is basically fake information, presented as being true. A person or government creates or shares disinformation to mislead, confuse or distract.

## HONEYPOT AFFAIR

When a person starts a romantic relationship with another person in order to find out secret information.

## ASSET

An asset is a secret source of intelligence – usually an agent.

## HANDLER

This is a sort of spy manager, and the person in charge of 'running' a specific agent or agents. They will be the agent's point of contact, and usually the person who passes information between the agent and the organization where the handler works.

## SPYMASTER

Someone who is a particularly great and effective spy. A very successful agent handler can sometimes be known as a spymaster.

## SECRET DOCUMENTS

These are papers or other kinds of records containing secret information that cannot be shared with anyone except those allowed to 'handle' them. (Being allowed to handle a document means that a person has permission to see that information, and help work out what to do with it.)

## LEAK

A leak means that somebody who was allowed to handle the information – and expected to keep it secret – has deliberately shared the information with others.

## BURNED

When a spy has been found out (or is about to be found out), and they are no longer able to work as a spy, they are said to have been burned. Often a burned agent will be 'cut off' from their bosses. In other words, they will never again be allowed to have any contact with the people who hired them to spy.

## CODE

A code is a way of disguising a message by replacing some – or all – of its words with letters or numbers, or a symbol of some sort.

## CRYPTOGRAPHY

This is the art of solving codes and revealing what they say.

## SLEEPER AGENT

A sleeper agent is a spy who is placed in one country by another country, but not used immediately. Instead, they must stay secret and be ready to act as a spy if and when needed.

## SECURITY

This is another way of saying *safety*, and it is a word that comes up a lot. Particularly 'national security', which means the safety of a specific country.

## INTERROGATION

This is when a person is questioned over and over by a country or organization in order to try to get information out of them. During an interrogation, a person might be threatened, or even physically hurt, to force them to reveal secrets.

## UNDERCOVER

When a person pretends to be someone else in order to go unnoticed while they spy.

## MOLE

A person who goes undercover among a group of people in order to find out information.

## CODE NAME

Not to be confused with an 'alias'. Both are secret names given to an agent. A spy might go undercover with an alias (say, 'Anna Chapman'). A code name is one used by the spy's handler and others they may meet, designed to hide the spy's identity (including their alias). For example, Noor Inayat Khan's code name was Madeleine, and her alias was Jeanne-Marie Renier. Sometimes a spy has several code names, or aliases.

# SPY AGENCIES

Around the world, there are countless organizations used for spying. Many countries have more than one. Some are so secret we might hardly – if ever – hear about them. I can't include them all, but here are some we will be mentioning in this book.

## GOVERNMENT COMMUNICATIONS HEADQUARTERS (GCHQ)

Using the latest, cutting-edge technology, GCHQ protects the UK from cyberattack. They need to be ready for *anything*. Attackers might try to hack into hospital computers to cause problems for doctors and patients. Or they might attack a website and share people's private information, such as bank details or passwords.

## THE SECURITY SERVICE (MI5)

The names MI5 and MI6 date back to the First World War, when they were part of the Directorate of Military Intelligence of the War Office. MI5 is based in the UK, where it detects threats to the country, such as terrorism and cyberattacks. Meanwhile, it monitors UK citizens (those living and working in the UK) while also keeping an eye on foreign spies who might steal top-secret information.

## SECRET INTELLIGENCE SERVICE (MI6)

MI6 does a similar job to MI5, but from outside the UK. By working in other countries, it protects the UK from foreign threats, such as terrorism, cyberattacks and enemy spies.

## FEDERAL BUREAU OF INTELLIGENCE (FBI)

In the USA, the FBI investigates threats to national security and federal crimes (each state in the USA sets its own laws, but a federal crime is one that is illegal across the entire country). The FBI also works to gather intelligence and assist other law enforcement agencies (such as the police) in order to defend the USA.

## CENTRAL INTELLIGENCE AGENCY (CIA)

The CIA collects intelligence in order to protect national security and stop any threats to the USA.

## NARODNY KOMISSARIAT VNUTRENNIKH DEL (NKVD)

This was once the Soviet Union's secret police. During the Second World War, the NKVD ran its spying operations and protected its borders. Between 1934 and 1946, the NKVD arrested, imprisoned, tortured and murdered hundreds of thousands of Soviet citizens.

## OFFICE FOR STRATEGIC SERVICES (OSS)

This was the USA's first proper intelligence organization. The OSS worked during the Second World War, but in September 1947 it became the model for the brand new Central Intelligence Agency (CIA).

## SPECIAL OPERATIONS EXECUTIVE (SOE)

This secret British organization was a sort of underground army. It operated during the Second World War, spying on – and sabotaging – its enemies. Working mainly in occupied countries (those under control of Nazi Germany and its allies) the SOE blew up trains and bridges and took part in armed combat. Both men and women were trained to be couriers, radio operators, **saboteurs** and spies.

# ELIZEBETH
# SMITH FRIEDMAN

How many people can say they have been experts in the works of Shakespeare *and* brought down dangerous criminals?

Elizebeth Smith Friedman had an exceptional life, by any standard. For a woman in the early twentieth century, at a time when women weren't treated as equal to men, it was particularly impressive.

A cryptanalyst (or codebreaker) in both the First and Second World wars, Elizebeth was born the youngest of ten children, on 26 August 1892, in Huntington, Indiana, in the United States. She studied English literature at college, and also read Latin, Greek and German. Though she didn't know it then, with these useful language skills she was setting herself up nicely for a career in codebreaking. This was a career that saw her working for the United States Treasury, the Coast Guard and the Navy, and bringing down **smugglers** around the world.

And it all started with a chance encounter.

After graduating from university, Elizebeth moved back home to help look after her parents and spent a brief spell working as a headteacher. One day, in 1916, she met a librarian who, on hearing about her interests and skills, got her a job at Riverbank, the United States' first ever organization for the study of cryptanalysis. That is, put simply: codebreaking.

There, Elizebeth met William Friedman, a fellow cryptanalyst and the man she would go on to marry. William is considered the founder of the National Security Agency (the US intelligence service), but it was his wife who introduced him to the art of codebreaking.

After Elizebeth retired, she and William published a book called *The Shakespearean Ciphers Examined*, which proved that Francis Bacon hadn't actually written the works of Shakespeare (as some people were claiming). This would have upset Colonel George Fabyan, the man who introduced

Elizebeth to cryptanalysis. You'll find out why when you read Elizebeth's story!

The world – and technology – had changed immeasurably by the time Elizebeth died, aged 88, on 31 October 1980, in New Jersey. But throughout her life, Elizebeth adapted brilliantly, both to new technology and to all the different jobs she'd had.

But before we discover Elizebeth's story, here's a conundrum for you to solve. Can you find the sentence hidden in the section below?

*So, are you any good at crosswords or codewords?*
*Hey, if you are, you could make a good cryptanalyst.*
*Each cryptanalyst must be able to crack codes with no*
*Information about how those codes were made.*
*Surely few have been better at this than the woman known as*
*America's first female cryptanalyst.*
*Secretly working in the world wars, she solved cases during*
*Prohibition in the United States, when alcohol was illegal.*
*You could say, she was pretty brilliant at cracking codes.*

ANSWER: SHE IS A SPY

E lizebeth never forgot the moment she first clapped eyes on that brilliant fool, Colonel George Fabyan.

For almost a year, while living back at home after graduating college, Elizebeth was in despair at what to do with her life. Her mother had always encouraged her to go her own way, and so she took a train to Chicago and stopped in at the library, looking for a job. There she got chatting to a librarian about her love of books. An hour or so passed and the librarian told her to stay right where she was, because they knew someone who might want to meet Elizebeth, and hire her to work at a private think tank – a place where big ideas are talked about and challenged. This think tank was in a 500-acre estate, in Geneva, Illinois. It was called the Riverbank Laboratories.

Well, it all sounded very intriguing to Elizebeth. A call was made – just like that – to the owner of Riverbank, one Colonel Fabyan, a man who had an interest in writing and language.

Colonel Fabyan was also passionate about Shakespeare. When he heard that Elizebeth was looking for a job, and was also interested in literature and Shakespeare, he showed up at the library and whisked her off to spend a weekend at his new Riverbank Laboratories.

Stepping into the train carriage with the Colonel that afternoon was like stepping into another world – and Elizebeth would never look back. Whatever might be said about Colonel Fabyan (and she'd said a few choice words over the years), that place was truly one of a kind. There were typists, translators, students of genetics and professionals specializing in acoustics engineering. To anyone else, it probably sounds horribly technical and boring, but Elizebeth came to realize that what they were doing there was exploring *ideas*. This included making, and breaking, codes. For quite a long time it was the only place in the United States doing this stuff.

Best of all, this new world would lead Elizebeth to William, her beloved husband and co-conspirator – though she didn't know it yet.

Everything Elizebeth could hope for from life was here, and all just an hour from the big lights of Chicago. Showing her around Riverbank, the eccentric Colonel Fabyan explained that

Elizebeth would be assisting Elizabeth Wells Gallup and her sister in the task of proving that Shakespeare hadn't written a word of his famous plays and sonnets. The Colonel introduced her to the theory – first published way back in the mid-19th century – that the great bard was in fact Sir Francis Bacon, the English philosopher and scientist.

Elizebeth had never heard such nonsense! In any case, Fabyan explained that the team were to prove this theory by decrypting coded messages he believed were hidden in Shakespeare's plays and poems.

Well, it did turn out to be nonsense (of course it did), but those early days at Fabyan's research centre were great fun. They'd study the letters of Shakespeare, looking for those secret messages, then go for a swim before eating delicious food, sometimes making late-night escapades in Fabyan's fancy car.

But the day William was brought in to work with Elizebeth was the day the true meaning of her life became clear.

Very quickly, she confided to William that whatever secret messages her fellow workers were claiming to have found in Shakespeare's work were nonsense. They were simply seeing what they *wanted* to see, finding clues where there were none. With Elizebeth's encouragement, William joined her in working on Colonel Fabyan's pet project and, suffice to say, the Colonel had no idea what he'd created in the pair. He couldn't have imagined that one day they would write the book that proved him and his ridiculous theories about Sir Francis Bacon quite wrong.

Of course, Elizebeth never meant him any disrespect. It seems remarkable, looking back, that the Riverbank played such an important role in the First World War. Almost all the US Army's cryptanalysis was done there, and Elizebeth and William were a big part in that, even though they were only in their mid-20s. How many married couples can say that, together, they worked to help change the course of a war? Let alone at such a young age? They were a dream team – listening in to enemy communications and looking for patterns and signs in their messages so they could crack their codes. Together, the pair could solve almost any code within just two hours.

Then they ran away to get married, even though their parents objected. In those days, it wasn't always accepted for people of different religions to marry, and Elizebeth's parents were **Quakers**, while William's were Jewish. But that couldn't stop them. They were true equals, at home and at work.

In 1918, though, William left to join the army and set off for France, working as the personal codebreaker for US Army big-wig General John J. Pershing. And Elizebeth's heart broke in two. She couldn't bear to stay at Riverbank and return to Colonel Fabyan's pet project (though he very much wanted her to!). Instead, she went home and looked after her widowed father.

Elizebeth resented that women codebreakers weren't allowed to be sent to the front lines of the war, but she didn't resent William going. As far as she was concerned, he was a genius. But that didn't change the fact that while he'd be writing important papers about codebreaking, she'd be at home – a champion swimmer stranded in the Sahara.

Yet Elizebeth always knew that if William could have taken her with him, he would have done in a heartbeat.

Besides, William returned to Elizebeth a year later, in 1919, and in 1921 they went to work together in the War Office. He was the chief cryptanalyst then, and she was his secretary. We can only imagine that, on occasions, she had to bite her tongue – having to work *for* William, rather than with him. But she didn't blame him personally. And when their children arrived, she stayed at home, not expecting to return to work anytime soon.

Then came **Prohibition**.

Looking back, it's a wonder the **government** of the USA ever expected to keep alcohol out of the country when it was still legal in Canada and Mexico. Of course there were criminals waiting to take advantage of the new law banning its sale. All the gangs had to do was smuggle it across the borders. And radio messages, sent in code, were all they thought they needed to pass secrets about where and how they were bringing alcohol into the United States.

They must have thought they were invincible. Didn't they get a shock? In three years, working practically on her own, Elizebeth cracked 12,000 secret messages for the Coast Guard. There were no computers in those days, of course, and Elizebeth had only the most basic mathematical training. But she had a certain kind of mind – one that understood and saw patterns, which is very important for codebreaking. As she told those fellows who tried to sell her a code-building system: 'Our office doesn't make 'em, we only break 'em.'

And didn't they just.

It always tickled Elizebeth to think about how the alcohol smugglers responded, hiring their own cryptographers (and paying them a lot more than she was paid) to make their coded messages more difficult to crack! Sadly for them, she didn't give up, and cracked all 50 of their codes.

It was curious to Elizebeth, to find herself becoming a regular name in the newspapers; to be brought in as an expert during trials, to be asked to describe how codebreaking works and explain the evidence she and her team had found to the court. She didn't flinch when lawyers for the Capone gang tried to say her evidence was unreliable. Instead, she stood up and gave the court a lesson in basic codebreaking, to explain what she had found, and proving that she knew her stuff.

After that performance, the newspapers couldn't get enough of her, and were always trying to get her to make comments for their articles. But Elizebeth was a busy woman.

By 1937, the mother-of-two was running a small team of cryptographers. Together they cracked their toughest conundrum, when they were asked by the Canadian police to break a code in Cantonese, a dialect of Chinese that Elizebeth couldn't read or speak. Police thought the codes were being used by a man they suspected of being a drug smuggler – a millionaire by the name of Gordon Lim. The code was complicated, especially because the letters had been rearranged or changed to help disguise the message. That made things hard enough, but there was something that made it harder still: Cantonese has a completely different script to English.

Elizebeth didn't give up easily, however. One by one her team abandoned the mission, but she was determined. So she asked a Chinese friend who spoke Cantonese to read the messages to her out loud. Once she heard the words spoken, she recognized sounds that seemed to be referring to the name of a boat involved in drug smuggling – and she knew she had the answer!

Perhaps Elizebeth's biggest achievement, though, was bringing down an enemy that would become known as the Doll Woman.

Velvalee Dickinson was a spy for Japan during the war, and one of the most notorious traitors in the history of the USA. She was also a woman – so you can imagine how much the newspapers loved that.

Velvalee used her doll shop as a front to send secret messages around the world. On one occasion she sent a letter to someone living in a country that was supposedly not taking sides in the war. It was February 1942, and she was writing from Portland, Oregon, to someone in Buenos Aires, Argentina. The letter mentioned a 'wonderful doll hospital' where she had sent 'three Old English dolls' for repairs, as well as 'fish nets' and 'balloons'. Elizebeth and her team studied this letter, and finally worked out that the 'dolls' were actually three warships and that the 'doll hospital' was a shipyard where repairs were made. They also realized that the phrases 'fishing nets' and 'balloons' gave away important information about the US Army and Navy on the West Coast of the United States.

Elizebeth could still remember how they all

felt when they realized that those codes revealed the US ship positioning and movements in Pearl Harbor, where an attack by the Japanese brought the US into the Second World War. Velvalee, as it turns out, was all too happy to help make the planned attack a reality.

Was it strange to Elizebeth to be mainly remembered as the wife of the great William Friedman? We'll never know for sure. But Elizebeth might have wondered how different things would be if she was a man. After all, in the Second World War she created ways to secretly communicate that were later used by the organization that became the CIA. And she was an important cryptanalyst in the organization that kept an eye on secret radio communications in South America, a place that was crucial to the defence of the USA.

Of course, when a group of South American spies were found out, all because of the work Elizebeth and her teams had done, the FBI claimed that victory as their own – as they had done repeatedly over the years. And Elizebeth had been sworn to secrecy under the Espionage

Act, so she couldn't put her hand up and say it was she who did it!

In any case, Elizebeth must have missed William terribly when he passed away, leaving her on her own. Perhaps, whenever she felt down, or lost without him, she remembered the cipher she cheekily hid in the pages of their book on Shakespeare – the sentence which, when decoded, read: '*I did not write the plays. F. Bacon.*' That would have made her laugh.

# TOOLS OF HER TRADE
## CRYPTANALYSIS

Encrypted messages are messages written in code that only those who have the key can understand. Today these range from the old-school favourite Pig Latin to WhatsApp. (If you're wondering what Pig Latin is, try asking yourself: *What's Igpay Atinlay?*) Cryptanalysis is a way of studying and understanding information hidden in codes.

In Elizebeth Friedman's day, technologies like the ones we have today were still unthinkable. But the work she and her husband William did on codebreaking – learning to recognize and understand patterns and hidden systems – is partly to thank for the creation of modern technology. Their work laid the foundations of some of our most important codebreaking and code-making systems.

ANSWER: WHAT'S PIG LATIN?

# HISTORY DECODED

## SECOND WORLD WAR

The Second World War began after the Nazis, led by Adolf Hitler, invaded Poland in September 1939. It was fought between the Allied and Axis forces. Britain, America and the Soviet Union were the main Allied forces, while Germany, Italy and Japan were the main Axis forces. But over the next six years, most countries of the world got involved until it became a truly world war. By the time peace was declared in 1945, 75 million people — including 40 million civilians — were dead.

# GLAMOROUS NEW YORK ESTATE AGENT IS RUSSIAN SPY!

Americans waking up on an otherwise ordinary summer's day have found their lives changed by earth-shattering news.

The friends and neighbours they thought they knew are in fact secret agents living in towns and cities across the United States.

The FBI have arrested ten Russian spies living undercover in the United States of America. This was a network of sleeper agents – spies who are placed in a country not to immediately gather information, but to be ready to spy if and when they are needed.

The ring of spies-in-waiting is being referred to as the 'Illegals Program'. This is because rather than working inside Russian embassies and military bases, as is usual for foreign spies, they were pretending to be ordinary people. The FBI is calling its investigation into the Illegals Program 'Operation Ghost Stories'.

Some of the spies were mothers who lived in the suburbs and worked as secretaries. Some were teachers.

What they all had in common was that they were Russians who had been planted there by a Russian spying organization – the SVR. They had been placed in the US with the intention of eventually handing information back to their Russian spymasters.

The youngest of the ten spies arrested, and surely the most glamorous, is Anna Chapman, a 28-year-old estate agent living in New York City. Formerly Anna Kushchenko, Ms Chapman got a new surname and passport after marrying a British man, who had no idea what he was really getting involved with.

How much useful information, if any, Chapman eventually managed to hand over to the Russian government has not been revealed by the FBI. But what *is* known is that the FBI have found evidence the spies were secretly passing information and money using old-school spy-craft. This included the use of invisible ink, and modern cryptographic software, which is a way of hiding messages in images posted on the internet.

Perhaps the strangest part of the Illegals Program is this: Russia isn't currently at war with the United States, and the two countries aren't even enemies.

What is clear is that you can never quite be sure if there's a spy in your midst.

# EDITH CAVELL

The execution of the British nurse Edith Cavell, by German soldiers, was a chilling moment in the First World War. At the time, the author of the Sherlock Holmes books, Sir Arthur Conan Doyle, said: 'Everybody must feel disgusted at the barbarous actions of the German soldiers in murdering this great and glorious specimen of womanhood.' And most did.

Cavell was born in December 1865 in Norfolk, England, and was executed for spying at a shooting range known as Tir National, in Brussels (the capital city of Belgium), in October 1915. She was a much-loved British nurse who famously encouraged those she trained at L'École Belge d'Infirmières Diplômées, in Brussels, to treat all wounded as equals – whether they were allies or enemies, British or German. More than a century later, she remains a national hero. Her memorial statue in central London is engraved with the words she spoke the night before she was killed by **firing squad**: *Patriotism is not enough. I must have no hatred or bitterness for anyone.*

Edith was 49 years old when she was found guilty of helping Allied soldiers escape from Belgium, which at that point was under control of Germany. Germany also claimed that Cavell had been involved in espionage, helping to pass information about the movement of the German army and their plans back to Britain. The British government always denied that she was a spy. They insisted she had no role in espionage and was completely innocent of the charges brought against her.

This was put in doubt when the former head of MI5, Dame Stella Rimington, revealed that secret documents showed Edith Cavell may well have understood that her friends were secretly passing information, as well as helping men to escape. It is not thought that Edith personally handed over information to the British government, but that she knew she was helping others to do so. We know for certain that some of those Edith Cavell helped to escape to Holland (which hadn't taken sides in the

First World War) had secret messages sewn into the fabric of their clothes.

Whether or not Edith was aware of her role as part of a network of spies is still being debated, and for that reason I have kept some of the details in this story vague. The problem with writing about spies is that we can never truly know what they did or didn't do. Even when we think we are being given the answers, we would be wise to question them.

We know for sure that some people worry claims of Edith Cavell being a spy might overshadow her life's work, as a nurse and as a human being: to help everyone, equally. What do you think?

It is almost midnight in Edith's prison cell on the outskirts of Brussels, and soon, they tell her, she will be killed by firing squad. She has been found guilty by the German **military court** of helping 200 Allied soldiers escape from occupied Belgium. For saving the lives of the men she treated at the Clinique in Brussels, and at the home of her friend Marie de Croÿ, she will pay with hers.

I don't imagine Edith regretted her actions. As far as she was concerned, every single man deserved to live.

When she closes her eyes, she is at peace. She is not afraid to die. She has seen death so often that it is not strange or fearful to her now. And she has her Christian faith to comfort her in these final hours. She will not feel scared or alone because she returns to her Lord with her conscience clean. She helped allies and enemies alike because it is her belief, as a nurse and a member of the Anglican Church, that any soldier must be treated and helped, friend or foe. Each man is a father, husband or son. As a nurse, Edith knew she must take no part in the quarrel – her work is for humanity, and this work knows no country's borders.

Though her life will end, she doesn't resent those who have called her a spy, because the men she treated were able to escape. Her only regret about her life ending now is that she won't live to see the return of peace. This conflict has been cruel and bloody – so many are dead – but the ten weeks she has spent here in **solitary confinement** has been a brief rest from the bloodshed and the horror.

Edith knew that in helping those men get to Holland she and her friends were putting their lives on the line. We can only imagine how nervous she was as they conducted their secret meetings at the clinic on the Rue de la Culture, fearful of who might be watching.

But what choice did they have?

She saw what she saw, and couldn't turn a blind eye.

Her prison cell feels a world away from her childhood – a time of innocence and happiness in a village near Norwich, where her father was the local vicar. He grew sick, and it was while looking after him that Edith realized nursing was her true calling. After that, she trained at hospitals in Manchester and London, where she was fortunate to work under Eva Luckes, the matron of the London Hospital.

Eva was following new rules for nursing, which had been set out by Edith's heroine, Florence Nightingale, and which were very different from what had come before. Florence thought nurses should focus not only on the physical needs of a patient (for instance, on an injury) but on their health more generally – making sure they were coping, comfortable and as happy as they could be. She believed it was the duty of a nurse to look at the needs of the patient as a whole. To watch and understand them, whether they were rich or poor.

Like Florence Nightingale, Edith also decided to give her life to nursing and not to marry. She is not one to put the interests of herself before others.

The first thing she saw when she entered Ms Luckes's office was a sign on the wall that read 'Patients Come First'. Edith liked the idea of that. She also wanted to help those who were helpless, hurt, and in need of medical care but unable to pay for it.

So in 1907, when she was offered a job at a new and revolutionary training school for nurses by

Dr Antoine Depage, Edith knew she had to take it. He was an important surgeon, and Edith respected his work. At a time when most nursing was carried out by nuns, Dr Depage had the idea of starting a training school for any woman who wanted to be a nurse. Now he wanted to bring Edith in as matron, in charge of the nurses on the ward.

Edith still remembers her first day as though it were only minutes ago. The school was at 149 Rue de la Culture, in Brussels, Belgium – a terraced house with large windows and a wrought-iron balcony. She could never have guessed at what it was to become, or the horrors she would face there, once war broke out.

Edith was tasked with creating a nursing school with living quarters, a laboratory and a classroom. At the time the building was terribly run-down and she and her team of nurses had barely any money, so the idea of creating somewhere Edith could train students who were arriving in just four weeks was rather terrifying. As well as overseeing repairs, she would have to write the lessons, design uniforms and find suitably trained instructors.

Well, thinking of Florence Nightingale and all that she had achieved, Edith stood in what would become her office, took a deep breath, picked

up a fallen chair, sat down and got to work. She
wrote to her old teacher, Eva Luckes, asking
her for help in finding French-speaking nursing
instructors. Perhaps she also spoke to God. It
was lucky that they both answered her calls.

It wasn't easy to convince some people
that opening a school for nurses who weren't
nuns was a good idea. These were going to be
*professionals* – nurses who actually got paid. Not
everyone liked the idea of **middle-class** women
taking on paid work. But when Elisabeth of
Bavaria, Queen of the Belgians, broke her arm
and hired a nurse trained at Edith's school, they
were given the benefit of the doubt.

Within a year, they were training nurses for
hospitals, schools and nurseries across the country.
It was tiring but highly rewarding work. When
Edith was training to be a nurse herself, a teacher
once remarked that she was often late and not to
be relied upon. So she made it her duty not to judge
or reprimand students in the same way, but to
approach education with kindness and warmth.

These had been important values in her
upbringing. Edith's parents might have been poor,

but they were rich in heart, always encouraging Edith, her two sisters and her brother. When war broke out in 1914, and Brussels fell to the forces of the Central Powers (the Austro-Hungarian Empire, the Ottoman Empire and Bulgaria), Edith was visiting family in London, but chose to return to Belgium. How could she not? Sometimes in life we have to do the right thing, even if the right thing is not the easiest.

Edith knew from the beginning what a risk she was taking, returning to Brussels. Because she was not just returning to be a nurse. She was going back to join the Belgian underground intelligence network: La Dame Blanche.

La Dame Blanche translates as 'The White Lady', a codename inspired by a German legend which said that the rulers of Germany would fall after the sudden appearance of a woman wearing white.

We don't know exactly how Edith was recruited to the spies who called themselves La Dame Blanche, but they were soon providing important information on the movements of the German army. And many of them were women.

They watched German trains passing through Belgium, day and night, and handed this information to British intelligence in Holland, using a number of methods. On one occasion, a midwife carried reports wrapped around the whale bones of her corset. Her job as a medic meant she was allowed to cross **military lines**, going into areas controlled by the Germans – which included Belgium, a country Germany had invaded at the start of the war. The German soldiers let the midwife cross the military line, not knowing that she was helping the Allies, the very people who were fighting to get Belgium back and stop the Germans advancing any further.

Edith had no desire to put her nurses in danger. So she kept a great many secrets from them. When members of La Dame Blanche conducted secret meetings at the clinic in Brussels, she pretended that they were patients or friends, and if any of her colleagues or students arrived unannounced, she had to think of excuses. She didn't like lying, but she had no choice.

One of Edith's greatest friends was Marie de Croÿ, the Belgian aristocrat and a fellow nurse. Marie's family castle, Château de Bellignies, is in a beautiful estate in a French forest. Edith and her fellow nurses used it as a hospital, and wounded soldiers were brought to them for treatment. From there, and from her training school in Brussels, she worked day and night.

One day, two British soldiers, who had escaped their German captors, found their way to the clinic, where Edith gave them food and shelter. After that, many more followed. In time, a so-called escape line was formed between Belgium and Holland: a network of people offering help and shelter to soldiers making their escape.

The de Croÿ house was like a maze, with rooms that had been used as prisons in medieval times. One of these rooms was called the 'Black Hole' – it sat below a staircase and was a great spot to hide the escapees from surprise inspections by German soldiers. It was also here that photographs were taken and used to create fake passports for the men, before brave guides escorted them out of Belgium, and into neutral Holland.

Alas, after just one year, two volunteers who had helped keep the escape line going were arrested. Five days later, Edith was also arrested and imprisoned in St Gilles Prison in Brussels. It is here that she now awaits her own fate, and where she prays for Marie, and the many others, who were arrested alongside her. Thankfully she has heard that Marie escaped the death penalty. Marie had tried to save them, claiming it was she and her brother who were solely responsible for hiding the men at their home. She was condemned to ten years' **hard labour** and sent to a prison at Siegburg in Germany. When Kaiser Wilhelm II offered to free her, she said no. She didn't want to be given special treatment just because her family was important. That is the sort of person Marie de Croÿ was.

Of course Edith had known for some time that the Germans were suspicious of what she was doing at the clinic. A man named Otto Mayer – a member of the German **secret police** – had come to Brussels in June 1915, to investigate Edith as a suspected enemy of Germany. That month he visited the clinic. Nothing was discovered, but Edith and many of her nurses were arrested and interrogated. They were eventually released, and it was then that Marie de Croÿ warned Edith that the Germans were closing in on their organization and begged her to stop what she was doing. But she couldn't. There were still soldiers who needed her help.

In the end it was a man within Edith's network who gave her up: Georges Gaston Quien. The way the German soldiers and secret police interrogated suspected spies was brutal and Georges agreed to aid them in exchange for his life. He disguised himself as an Allied soldier who needed Edith's help getting out of the country and made his way to the clinic. All we know then is that Georges was helped to 'escape' to safety in June, and on 5 August, the German authorities entered the clinic and arrested Edith for hiding Allied soldiers.

Georges was later convicted by a French court as a collaborator – someone working with the enemy – and sentenced to death. Edith would feel no sense of justice in that, though. An eye for an eye was never her way.

At the time of our story, it is a year since Britain declared war on Germany. After Edith's arrest, she was truthful. She told her captors that she had helped 60 British soldiers, 15 French soldiers, and around a hundred more French and Belgian citizens. Some of them she offered a safe haven at her clinic, and others she helped to travel out of the country, unnoticed.

It's likely that the German forces want to make an example of Edith, to use her execution as a warning to anyone who might challenge their authority and help others in the face of danger.

As far as Edith is concerned, only the Lord knows what she did and who she truly is. And she is at peace with both.

Soon they will come for her. She is neither afraid nor angry, because she gives her life to her country. But she knows now that patriotism is not enough. She must have no hatred or bitterness for anyone.

# TOOLS OF HER TRADE
## FAITH

To my mind, Cavell made an excellent spy because of her faith – faith in Christianity, and faith in the kind of nurse, and person, she wanted to be. She had very clear morals, which meant that the most important thing for her was to help people no matter the personal cost, be that by making them better or by helping them escape danger.

## HISTORY DECODED
### FIRST WORLD WAR

The First World War (1914–1918) was a long, tedious, bloody, muddy war, triggered by the assassination of just one man – Archduke Franz Ferdinand, the heir to the throne of Austria-Hungary. Despite being called a 'world war', it was really a war between the Allied forces – including France, Britain, Russia, the

United States, Italy and Japan — and the Central Powers of Germany, the Austro-Hungarian Empire, the **Ottoman Empire** and Bulgaria. Much of the fighting took place on battlefields in which soldiers dug trenches to protect themselves and where the enemy trenches might be just 30 metres away. Each side launched attacks on the other in an attempt to advance, but in reality no one moved very far. Millions died. Fighting ceased at the eleventh hour of the eleventh day of the eleventh month in 1918, when a peace treaty was signed between Germany and the victorious Allies.

*29 APRIL 1992*

# BRITAIN GETS FIRST FEMALE HEAD OF MI5!

It is a day of double-firsts, as Dame Stella Rimington becomes both the first woman to be put in charge of MI5, and the first Director General of MI5 whose name will be made known to the public.

As the Director General, it is Dame Stella's job to oversee the whole running of the Security Service, otherwise known as MI5. She becomes responsible for producing the report that tells the government what MI5 has been working on each year. (This is then presented to the Home Office, the government department in charge of keeping the UK safe.)

Dame Stella's appointment comes decades after that of the first ever female MI5 officer. Jane Sissmore was just 18 years old when she was recruited into MI5, in 1916, and was promoted to become an MI5 officer in 1929. It was Sissmore (whose achievements also include training to become a barrister in her spare time!) who first put together clues about a British double agent working as a journalist – a description that fitted the Cambridge Five spy, Kim Philby. Unfortunately, she was sacked for refusing to obey orders before she ever managed to prove her theory about the identity of the Third Man.

To increase openness in the service, Dame Stella has announced plans to make secret files from the past available to read at the National Archives, in London – files that will help shed light on people like Jane Sissmore.

Having grown up in England during the Second World War, Dame Stella knows what it is like to live through conflict. During the **Blitz** bombings, she witnessed windows blown out and buildings caved in.

Her first job, before becoming a spy, was as an archivist – someone who organizes and looks after historical documents. After she married, Dame Stella moved to India with her husband. It was in India that she got the 'tap on the shoulder', which is spy speak for an invitation to work for the Secret Service. At first, this was as a typist, taking notes on meetings and conversations.

That was in 1967. In the following decades, Dame Stella went on to work in lots of different roles, including counter-subversion, which involves outsmarting people or groups working against the British government. She also worked in counter-terrorism, trying to stop anyone causing harm to UK citizens.

As they say: there ain't nothing like a dame!

# HARRIET TUBMAN

Harriet Tubman was the most famous conductor on the Underground Railroad. This was not an actual railroad, but a group of people in the United States who worked together to help enslaved people escape from slavery. She was also a brilliant spy. In fact, Harriet was one of the most important people in the American Civil War. This was a war fought in the United States between the Confederates in the south of the country and the Unionists in the north. The main thing the north and south were fighting about was slavery, which the Confederate South wanted to keep and expand, and the Unionist North wanted to limit and (eventually) end. When the war broke out, Harriet, a Black woman who had been born into enslavement but had freed herself and hundreds of others, fought for the Unionists and for the freedom of all Black people.

The enslavement of African and African-descended people in the British North American Colonies and the US (the United States of America became its own country in 1776) lasted from 1619 until 1865. It began with the arrival of twenty Africans who were brought to Virginia, a British Colony on the Atlantic coast, aboard an English ship sailing under a Dutch flag.

Then, from the mid-seventeenth century, British, American and other European traders bought and enslaved African people in larger numbers, forcing them to work on plantations, in cities, shipyards and basically anywhere work needed to be done. Britain banned the international slave trade in 1807, and the United States banned the importation of enslaved people in 1808. But legal enslavement continued in the British Caribbean colonies until 1833, and in the US until the end of the American Civil War in 1865. Before then, European traders captured, enslaved and trafficked more than 12 million African men, women and children across the vast Atlantic Ocean. Many countries participated in and made money from this horrific trade in human beings, including Britain, the United States, Portugal, Spain, Brazil, France and the Netherlands.

This period was absolutely brutal. Enslaved people were treated viciously. They were subjected to terrible violence and humiliation, and could not legally marry. The children of enslaved women were born enslaved, and enslavers often sold children away from their families, leaving parents with no idea where their children had gone or if they would ever see them again.

Ever since the United States fought a war with Great Britain to become its own country in 1776, there had been disagreement between the north and the south of the United States about slavery and what role it would play in the country's future.

Tensions grew as the decades wore on, and in the early hours of 12 April 1861, Confederates opened fire in the harbour of Charleston, South Carolina, and started what would become the American Civil War – one of the deadliest conflicts in the history of the United States. It ended in 1865, when Confederate troops in the south surrendered to the Unionists in the north.

During the war, Harriet was the first woman to lead an attack against the enemy. She was also a remarkable scout – a spy who is 'the eyes and ears' of their commander during a battle. It was the job of scouts like Harriet to track the enemy, and report on their movements and plans.

Harriet was born Araminta Hall, though everyone knew her as Minty. Like many enslaved people, Harriet's birthday was not properly recorded but we know she was born into slavery in 1822, in Maryland, USA. From an early age, she was made to do exhausting, often dangerous, and of course unpaid work in the fields: setting traps for animals, hauling logs and driving oxen.

In 1849, Harriet escaped from slavery. Then, through sheer bravery and dedication, she went on to help free hundreds of enslaved people. As her reputation grew, she became known as 'the Moses of Her People'. Harriet died on 10 March 1913, in Auburn, New York, in her early nineties, in a care home she had helped set up for elderly African Americans.

Harriet had played a crucial role at a very important point in history. But after everything she did to help others, she still had to fight to get a **pension** for her services during the American Civil War, while the men she fought alongside automatically received theirs, as thanks for their service.

Why do you think that might have been?

When you're born an enslaved person, your life is not your own.

Harriet and her family members were moveable property, legally belonging to someone else. A couple named Eliza and Edward Brodess owned Harriet (who was then called 'Minty'), along with her mother, brothers and sisters. Her mother looked after the Brodess family's big house, and so didn't have much time for Harriet and her younger brother, or the baby. Looking after them fell to Harriet, even though she was still just a little girl herself.

When Harriet was only five years old, the Brodess family hired her out as a housemaid and nursemaid to a woman Harriet would have called 'Miss Susan', who lived a little way away. Miss Susan wasn't a kind lady. It was Harriet's job to rock Miss Susan's baby to sleep, and when her baby cried it was Harriet who got the beating.

Harriet fought back. One day, she was beaten for stealing a sugar cube. She tried running away, hiding out in a pigsty for four days. When the threat of starvation forced her to return, she learned to wear thick layers of clothes to protect against Miss Susan's sting.

Some violence, though, she couldn't be ready for. When she was 13, Harriet was hit in the head by a 2 lb metal weight. An overseer was trying to catch an enslaved man who was attempting to escape. When Harriet refused to help the overseer, he threw a metal weight at the fleeing man, but Harriet got hit instead. She was badly injured, and her skull was cracked, but she survived. From then on, though, she suffered painful headaches and seizures and blackouts. She also had strange, vivid dreams. This period was one of the worst of her life; but she might say that, in a strange way, it was also the best. For out of that pain, Harriet found God. Hers was the God of the Old Testament, who spoke to the prophet Moses, who parted the Red Sea and led the Israelites out of Egypt, and out of bondage.

In 1844, Harriet met a free Black man by the name of John Tubman. She got permission from Edward Brodess to marry John, but things were complicated. Even though John was not enslaved, if he and Harriet had children together, their children would have been enslaved – just like Harriet.

That wasn't to be, though. Five years after John and Harriet married, Edward died. Harriet knew what was coming. As soon as he got sick, Harriet heard his wife, Eliza, talking about how she needed to raise money to pay off her husband's debts. Harriet knew then that she would be sold off, and that she would have no say in where she might end up. Around the same time that she suffered the blow to her head, Edward had sold three of Harriet's sisters – Linah, Soph and Mariah Ritty – in other states, and Harriet never saw them again.

After Edward Brodess died, Harriet couldn't just wait around to be separated forever from the people she loved. There was nothing for it but to escape. It was then that she changed her name from Minty to Harriet, after her mother, and took her husband's surname.

By the time she escaped north, at the grand age of 27, she was Harriet Tubman. Minty Hall had vanished into thin air.

Just before her escape, Harriet had been hired out to a man in neighbouring Caroline County. She had saved enough money for the journey, and left in the dead of night, following the North Star.

Immediately, Eliza Brodess put out a $100 reward for her capture.

Harriet had to move quickly, knowing what would happen if she got caught. She had found that trusting anyone was a risk, but she had no choice. The first person to help her was a white Quaker woman, who gave Harriet shelter for the night.

From there, she used various disguises to stay hidden, sometimes carrying a couple of chickens, as though she was just another person working in the fields. One time, fearing she would be discovered by a man she recognized, Harriet let go of the chickens she was carrying. Running fast after them, she pretended they had escaped, using it as a ruse to get away from the man as quickly as possible.

It worked. She heard him laugh when he saw Harriet, but he never recognized her.

Harriet continued on foot and train, and sometimes horse and wagon, making the 90-mile journey north with the help of the Underground Railroad, which was a secret group who helped other escapees stay out of sight. These people offered shelter, support and aid, and helped Harriet flee from Maryland to Philadelphia, in the free northern state of Pennsylvania, where she would be safe.

Harriet's faith helped, too. When she found she had crossed that line to safety in Philadelphia, she looked at her hands to see if she was the same person who had left Maryland. It seemed unbelievable that she had made it. Instantly, she felt like everything had changed.

Once she was free, Harriet did not rest. Instead, she spent the next 10 years helping free others via the Underground Railroad, taking secret trips between the north and south. It was incredibly dangerous for anyone to be caught helping enslaved people, so the Underground Railroad used a sort of code to talk in secret. The homes where runaways would stay and eat were called 'stations' or 'depots', and the so-called 'conductor' was the person responsible for moving runaways from one place to another. The homeowners of these stations were called 'stationmasters'. Harriet is the most well-known of all the conductors who ever worked on this Railroad.

It was illegal to teach an enslaved person to read or write, so the Underground Railroad had to find new inventive ways to communicate with people who couldn't read secret messages. Through singing they managed to organize and pass messages across the fields, and along the Underground Railroad network. They had signal songs, which gave directions on how to escape, and map songs, which provided details of meeting points.

There were lanterns placed in front of safe houses, and a code for knocking on the doors of those houses, so runaways could tell the residents who they were.

Harriet returned to Maryland many times, guiding her family and others to freedom. She helped around 70 people in total, and never lost a passenger:

'I was the conductor of the Underground Railroad for eight years, and I can say what most conductors can't say – I never ran my train off the track and I never lost a passenger.' (Tubman's Address to a Suffrage Convention, New York, 1896)

It wasn't always easy, though. Harriet had to give a sedative (a calming drug) to a baby once to stop it crying, and on another occasion she had to hold a gun to a man who got spooked and tried to turn back. She couldn't risk him being tortured and telling their enemies details of the Underground Railroad, so she threatened to kill him if he ran. Like she told him: dead folk tell no tales.

Harriet had believed she and John would be together again when she returned south. She had even bought a new suit to wear for the occasion. But when the time came, she found he'd remarried. Harriet's heart was broken, but she kept calm and tried not to blame him. Maybe he'd struggled to believe that she was still alive.

Eight years after she had freed herself, on one of her dangerous missions to Maryland, Harriet organized the escape of her parents and siblings. Getting her elderly father to freedom was her greatest challenge. Harriet had no choice but to take a train (an actual train this time!) in broad daylight, even though there was a bounty on her head – a reward of money for anyone who caught her. This was the spring of 1857, and once Harriet reached Caroline County she got herself a horse and, with spare parts, made a buggy to transport her father. It worked, and Harriet got him and her

mother to safety in Canada with the help of a
trusted friend in the Underground Railroad.

Over the years, Harriet conducted 13 journeys
on the Underground Railroad and brought around
70 people to freedom. But despite her incredible
feats, Harriet could not save all her family members.
There were the three sisters she never saw again.
And while she managed to help free her four
brothers – Ben, Robert, Henry and Moses – she
failed to rescue her beloved sister, Rachel, or Rachel's
two children. Rachel died in 1859, before Harriet
could rescue her. And her death made Harriet even
more determined to fight, in whatever way she could.

It was in Canada that Harriet met John Brown,
a white American man who was determined to do
everything he could to end slavery.

Harriet felt that she had already met John in
a dream, and John was in awe of Tubman and
all she had accomplished. She agreed to help
him organize what would become known as the
Harpers Ferry Raid. This was an attack on the
armoury at Harpers Ferry, Virginia – a place
where the United States government stored and
made weapons for the army.

The raid came in 1859, just before the start
of the Civil War, and was an attempt to create

a revolution throughout the southern states of America and end slavery for good. And the organizers truly believed that it would. But on the day of the attack, things didn't go as planned. Sickness meant Harriet couldn't be there when John and his men made their attack. Chances are, if she had been, she would not have survived. Of the 22 men who took part, 10 were killed and five escaped. The other seven, including John Brown himself, were captured, then later executed for their part in the raid.

Shortly after the outbreak of the Civil War, in 1861, Harriet joined the Union Army, volunteering for duty at Fort Monroe in Virginia. Harriet was assigned to work as scout and spy fighting against the Confederates, but she worked as a nurse and a cook as well. She also helped enslaved people who had escaped, and were living in Union camps as refugees. She helped these people find ways to support themselves, and recruited some as scouts.

Disguising herself as someone working on land owned by Confederate enemies, Harriet hid behind enemy lines, leading missions to find the locations of Confederate mines and troops. And she delivered this information back to her fellow

Unionists. The Confederation didn't know that right under their noses, scouts were gathering the facts that would help the Union Army free their people.

There is so much to make Harriet proud as she looks back at her life. And perhaps the proudest moment of all is her role in what became known as the Combahee Ferry Raid. The plan for the raid was to remove deadly explosive mines from the Combahee River in South Carolina, seize supplies from plantations in the area, free the enslaved people working on them and then destroy the plantations themselves. And boy, did the Unionists do it!

It was here that Harriet became the first woman of any race to lead a military operation in the United States. In the raid, Harriet led 150 Black soldiers of an army regiment called the 2nd South Carolina Infantry. Together, they freed more than 750 enslaved people. Many of them then joined the Union Army and fought for freedom.

After the war, Harriet married a war veteran 20 years younger than her, called Nelson Davis.

Harriet always lived close to her family and helped raise her eight siblings' children and grandchildren. In 1874 Harriet and Nelson adopted a daughter, Gertie Davis. Nelson and Gertie both died young, but Harriet lived into her nineties.

She took comfort in what she did for her nieces and nephews. She also worked tirelessly up to her final years to promote women's suffrage – the right for women to vote in elections and have a say in how the country is run.

A woman once asked Harriet whether she believed women ought to have the vote. Harriet's response? *I suffered enough to believe it.*

# TOOLS OF HER TRADE
## HIDING IN PLAIN SIGHT

Enslaved and formerly enslaved people made excellent scouts because their enemies were the people who kept them in bondage. This meant the scouts could hide in plain sight as they carried out their daily work, reporting on what the Confederates were saying and planning. Working together, the Union spies were able to listen in and gather intelligence from behind Confederate enemy lines, where they were working for their slave masters. This was information that would help the Union Army to find the locations of Confederate mines, supply areas and troops.

# BREAKING NEWS: US SPY IS DOUBLE-AGENT FOR CUBA!

The United States is still recovering from the shock of the 9/11 terrorist attacks, where nearly 3,000 people died. But just ten days later, a new threat to America has emerged in the form of a Cuban spy named Ana Belén Montes . . .

Until this week, Montes played an important role in the US Defense Intelligence Agency. Her speciality was Cuba, the communist island country that sits where the northern Caribbean Sea, Gulf of Mexico and Atlantic Ocean meet, and which has famously been at odds with the US since the Cold War. Montes' work on the country was so important that she was known by her colleagues as the Queen of Cuba.

But in a twist worthy of a Hollywood movie, an investigation by the FBI has revealed that Montes, 44, has in fact been a double agent all along. For 17 years, she has been working as a Cuban spy, leaking top-secret information about the US Army.

Montes' family is from the Caribbean island of Puerto Rico, but she grew up in the

United States, where her father was a psychiatrist and a former colonel in the US Army. Both her brother and sister work for the FBI. Her sister even helped discover a group of Cuban spies in Miami.

With her family's connections to trusted US organizations, it's hardly surprising that Montes has remained undetected for so long, especially as she covered her tracks amazingly well. While double-crossing the US government, it's been revealed that Montes never stole any documents. Instead, she memorized details she saw at the office and later typed them up on her laptop at home, before transferring the information from her computer onto encrypted discs.

Instructions from her Cuban bosses would be communicated via a short-wave radio Montes kept in her wardrobe. These messages provided details of where and when to meet her Cuban handler and pass over the discs loaded with top-secret information.

To discover how Montes' life as a double agent began, we need to go back to 1984, when she took an ordinary job at the Department of Justice (an important government department) in Washington. There, Montes spoke openly about how she hated the

US government's attitude towards Central America.

From the late 1970s onwards, Central America was often the backdrop for civil wars and communist revolutions. These happened because local people were unhappy with the unfair way they were treated by foreign countries and businesses. Meanwhile, the Cold War was in full swing and the US was worried that if communist governments won power in Central America, this would give the Soviet Union a huge advantage and cut off South America from North America.

Central America soon became a battleground in a proxy war. This happens when major powers fund others to fight on their behalf, instead of fighting themselves. This proxy war was between the United States and the Soviet Union. In Nicaragua, the US backed a group of rebels known as the Contras (a name that means 'counter-revolution'), while the Soviet Union and Cuba backed the group that claimed to have communist ideals.

Ana Belén Montes knew about this proxy war all too well. Her heart lay with Cuba and the communist revolutionaries, a feeling that she didn't hide, even though she was now working in the offices of the US government. Soon, her opinions caught the attention of Cuban leaders, who thought she could be useful to them. And they were right. After being approached by a member of the Cuban government, Montes agreed to spy for Cuba. In 1985, she applied for a job in the United States Defense Intelligence Agency, and soon worked her way up the ranks, all the while living another life as a full-blown double agent.

But in the end, she couldn't keep up the lie.

Montes' colleagues grew suspicious after learning of her views about Central America. At first, she passed a lie detector test and was allowed to continue with her job. But now, a year after suspicious colleagues first tipped them off, the FBI have made their arrest.

Ana Belén Montes accepted no money for passing information to Cuba. Her reason for spying was based purely on her ideas and values – because she didn't approve of how the US was behaving in other countries.

It is thought that Montes gave away information so secret that it could not even be revealed to the FBI special agent who led the investigation into her.

# MATA HARI

Mata Hari's story is extraordinary in lots of ways. A famous dancer, who was known for trying to seduce men, she was executed as a spy for Germany during the First World War in 1917.

But this is only part of her story. Mata Hari had many secret lives.

Her real name was Margaretha Geertruida Zelle. Born in the Netherlands in 1876, she later became a renowned exotic dancer – someone who removes pieces of their clothing while performing. Both of Margaretha's parents were Dutch and she grew up in the Netherlands. She thought that if her audience knew who she really was, she might seem boring. So, to make herself more interesting, Margaretha convinced everyone (including newspaper writers) that she was of Indian descent and that she had been taught these ancient dances by a priestess.

The way Mata Hari's story has been told over the years reveals a lot about how certain women have been treated in the past. Mata Hari has often been dismissed as a *femme fatale*. This is a woman who supposedly makes helpless men fall in love with her, using her irresistible charm and beauty to take advantage. For a long time, Mata Hari was remembered as someone who used her dancing to seduce men and then steal their secrets.

But more often than not, when you look into stories of *femmes fatales*, rather than finding a powerful predator taking advantage of helpless men, you find a woman who had no money or power, and was simply using what was available to her in a world that has treated her unfairly. The reason Mata Hari worked so hard as a dancer is that she was desperately trying to save up money to be reunited with her daughter, Louise Jeanne. Unless she was able to support her daughter in the same way that Louise Jeanne's father could, Mata didn't think it was fair to look after her.

Her own childhood had not been very happy. Margaretha was the eldest of four children. After their family lost all their money, her parents divorced, and then her mother died in 1891, when Margaretha was just 15. Her father remarried in Amsterdam and the family fell apart. In an attempt to make a new life for herself, Margaretha went to live with her godfather and trained as a nursery teacher. When the headmaster of the school she worked at started to flirt with her, she fled and went to live at her uncle's home in the Hague, in Holland.

By this time, Margaretha was approaching adulthood. At the age of 18, she answered a 'lonely hearts' newspaper advert – people used to place these in newspapers to find potential romantic partners. This was from an officer in the East Indies army (the East Indies is a term historically used by the Dutch and other European countries for a large group of islands they had colonised in the Indian and Pacific Oceans). He was almost twice her age, and – it turns out – drank too much alcohol. However, just four months later, Margaretha married the officer, named Rudolph 'John' MacLeod, and they moved to Java in Indonesia and had two children. Tragically, both children were believed to have been poisoned by a member of staff – possibly in revenge for their father's attack on a young local woman – and their son, Norman, died as a result.

After this, Margaretha and her cruel husband moved back to Europe and then separated. Rudolph kept their daughter, Louise Jeanne, also known as Non (Margaretha called her Nonnie), refusing to give Mata any money.

As a spy, Mata Hari's story is shrouded in further mystery. Because she was Dutch, and the Netherlands was neutral in the First World War, she was allowed to move back and forth over the borders between countries, which most people weren't. This made her useful to both sides in the war — the Allies and Central Powers — as a possible spy.

Some say that while living in the Hague she was paid by the Germans to find out whatever information she could during her next visit to France and report it back to them. Years later, after she was arrested by the French, Mata admitted that she had accepted money from Germany, but said she had only given them outdated information, which wouldn't be of any use.

Others say she wasn't an incredible German spy, but was instead used by France as a **scapegoat** – a distraction from the country's own failings in the war. In 1917, the French army had suffered **mutinies** and the Allies (including the UK and

France) believed they were about to lose the war. An author called Léon Schirmann thought that the spotlight had been turned on Mata Hari to save face and protect France's reputation. She was the 'perfect victim', he said, because she was foreign, so many believed she could indeed be a spy. And as an exotic dancer who had many boyfriends she had a reputation for being 'immoral'. She was presented by France as a woman who had been enjoying a fancy lifestyle while the soldiers and people of France were suffering terribly.

When the French authorities arrested Mata Hari for espionage in February 1917, and imprisoned her at Saint-Lazare Prison in Paris, she was accused of revealing details of the Allied forces' new weapon: the tank. The fact that the Germans found out about the tank resulted in the loss of many lives, and possibly prolonged the war. Mata Hari was also accused of helping to direct Allied ships towards their enemy's U-boats, which prowled the Atlantic armed with torpedoes. This may have directly caused the deaths of at least fifty thousand soldiers.

But there are those who say she was largely innocent of these crimes. And as they point out, neither one of these accusations came up at her trial.

Mata Hari's private letters were put on display a few years ago, at an exhibition in her hometown. These make it clear that Mata Hari desperately wanted to be reunited with her daughter, Nonnie. Sadly, she never was, and Nonnie died of a brain haemorrhage two years after her mother's death.

Whatever the truth, Mata Hari's story shows us that, in war, few things are black and white . . .

A lot of tall stories were told about Mata's life after she'd gone. But perhaps only those closest to her knew the truth.

As an exotic dancer, she might have told a few white lies . . . That she was born in a sacred Indian temple. That she was given the name Mata Hari, meaning 'eye of the day', by a priestess.

And what's the harm in a little make-believe? Are they any different to the stories Mata used to read to her daughter, Nonnie, when she was young? Everybody loves a fairy tale, and dance is a performance. In the end, what is more entertaining – to watch a woman like Mata dance routines, believing they were inspired by a childhood in India? Or to know that she was just plain old Gretha, born in a small town in the Netherlands.

The truth is that she danced because she had to.

The story told at Mata's trial was riddled with lies. History is full of women who supposedly manipulated and controlled men through their powers of **seduction**. And perhaps men really are so weak.

Or perhaps it is easier to think of women having mystical power than it is to blame these men for being so stupid – or to blame a society where women have to behave like Mata has, in order to protect her child. Nonnie's father was violent, and after he took her away from Mata, Mata did all that she could to survive, and to make a world that she and her daughter could live in, together.

When the French executed Mata, they called her a German spy. But the truth of her story is this . . .

Mata's father did everything he could to give her a great education. In the end, though, his wealth fell away. After Mata's mother died, when she was just 15, she was separated from her brothers and sent away to live with relatives. Determined to see the world and to make something of her life, she was 18 when she answered an advert in a Dutch newspaper placed by Nonnie's father. At that time he was an officer in the Dutch colonial army, and he was looking for a wife.

Four months later, Captain Rudolf MacLeod and Mata were married and they travelled together to what was then the Dutch East Indies, in Southeast Asia, which is where Mata picked up the dancing knowledge that would prove so useful.

Rudolph was not a good man. He drank too much, and it was when he drank too much that he became violent. Mata never regretted her marriage to him, though, as together they had Nonnie and her brother, Norman. Mata's children were the best thing that happened in her life – she couldn't believe her luck when they came along.

But it is harder still to believe that the person she trusted to look after Nonnie and her brother did the worst thing imaginable. When they were young, for reasons Mata could never fathom, the nanny looking after Nonnie and Norman poisoned them both. Norman died, and Nonnie survived. But not without suffering . . .

Mata still thinks about Nonnie's suffering. As if losing her brother like that wasn't enough, she also contracted syphilis, an infection caused by bacteria, which Nonnie's father had passed on to Mata who had, in turn, passed it on to Nonnie. The mercury treatment they gave Nonnie didn't work and Mata felt helpless. It is difficult to imagine what it must have been like, not to be able to keep your child safe.

Nonnie's father was unpredictable. One afternoon, in a fearful rage, he came close to murdering Mata with a bread knife. Thankfully, a chair fell on the floor between them, giving her time to get to the door and find help. You can see why Mata had to leave.

She desperately wanted to take Nonnie with her, but hadn't the money to look after her daughter, and Nonnie's father refused to pay any child support. So she had no choice. Mata would surely have done anything to stay with Nonnie but she feared if she stayed, Nonnie's father would kill her. From then on, she made it her mission to make enough money so that she could get Nonnie back and look after her.

In Paris, Mata worked as a piano teacher, a dancer and an artist's model, posing naked for paintings and drawings, hoping to earn enough to be reunited with her Nonnie. Crossing borders, she worked the dance halls of the world, making a name for herself – the name of Mata Hari – and becoming well-known for her performances, which transported those who watched her to another world. When she danced, she too was briefly able to forget everything that had happened to her. Whether selling out dance halls in Madrid or in Paris, when she danced Mata could imagine she was someone new; someone who hadn't lost the one person she had left in this world.

But Mata had started performing late in life, and by the time she reached her thirties she was old for a dancer, and fewer people were coming to see her. In 1913, her dancing career went into decline. Nonnie was 15 by then and Mata began to fear they would never be reunited. To make ends meet, she took work as a courtesan – providing company to men in return for money. In her case, these men were usually important military officers and politicians, often from different countries. This gave her an edge. When the war broke out Mata was able to access secrets from both sides: plans and information about the movement of armies and troops. But the truth was, she never planned to be a spy.

Mata was in Berlin, Germany, when war was declared. The troops there stole her money and her fur coats and told her to return to the Netherlands. But two years later she was approached by the Germans, who offered her 50,000 francs to go to Paris and spy on the French. Perhaps they thought that because she was still travelling a bit for her dancing, and because she had relationships with important officers, she would be able to get them the information they needed in a way that others couldn't. Maybe they thought a woman can get a man to tell her anything if she bats her eyelids in the right way. And perhaps Mata agreed with them. She certainly agreed to do it, most likely because she needed the money. She might also have reckoned that, with her looks and her charm, she could take the money from Germany, but get away without doing much actual spying.

For the next couple of years, that was what she did. Twice she went to France, and as the evidence in her trial showed, the French agents who were following her at the time didn't catch her doing anything worth reporting.

While she was in France, she fell in love. He was a young Russian officer, Vadim Maslov, and the only man Mata had ever really cared for. She only wished Nonnie could have met him.

Several times in 1916, Georges Ladoux, the French counter-intelligence chief (a person who catches the spies), contacted Mata and tried to persuade her to spy for his side, instead of the Germans. She said no, no, no – until, finally, she said yes. She agreed to go to Belgium, where she would seduce important German officers and find out their secrets, in return for a million francs (a *huge* amount of money in those days). This way she thought she could settle down with Vadim and give up her other paying lovers, and perhaps still be reunited with her Nonnie.

You can see why both sides wanted Mata to work for them. Mata was Dutch, and she could move more easily from one country to another. This was because the Netherlands was a neutral country during the war. This made her useful to both the French and the Germans, who each wanted to take advantage of her freedom.

The stories of Mata's life have many different versions of who she spied for and why. Some will say she was a German spy. Others will say she was a double agent, pretending to spy for Germany while secretly working for the French.

Possibly Mata didn't see herself as either. She was a person trying to survive, the best way she knew how. She thought she could play both sides. But she was wrong.

Among her lovers was a Major Arnold Kalle, the German military attaché (an army officer working for the German embassy), who threw her to the wolves.

Major Kalle must have suspected Mata was working for the French, at the same time the French began to suspect she was working for the Germans. So, one day, he sent her messages using a code that he knew the French had already broken and could read. Sure enough, the French intercepted the message and thought they had caught a spy.

She was arrested in a luxury hotel room in Paris.

That was February 1917. During her trial, five months later, Mata was blamed for the deaths of 50,000 French soldiers. And yet no actual evidence was shown as to how she had caused these deaths.

Was she guilty? From the start the French judge certainly seemed to want her to be guilty. She was an immoral woman, he said, and had no respect for the people of France or their suffering. On 25 July that year, she was indeed found guilty of espionage – and the Dutch government did nothing to help her.

The next day, after months of starvation, and being held in a cell infested with rats, they would shoot Mata.

People believe what they want to believe. Does it matter if she was not a real spy, but a woman with few options left, doing what she needed to do to survive? Or that she danced as a way to bring joy and to distract herself from the loss of her children? That she had relationships with men in order to make enough money to be with her daughter again?

Perhaps *what* she did, and for whom, is less important than *why* she did it: to return to her Nonnie . . .

# TOOLS OF HER TRADE
## POLITICAL NEUTRALITY

The Netherlands was one of the few countries that didn't take sides in the First World War. Because Mata Hari was Dutch, she was allowed to cross borders between Allied and Axis countries, such as France and Germany. Given that she was a performer, she often travelled, so it didn't seem suspicious for her to go from one country to another. This made her valuable to both sides, each of whom wanted to use her as a spy. It seemed Mata Hari accepted offers from Germany and France, to spy for each on the other, and paid for her choices with her life.

# 'MAKER OF KINGS' GERTRUDE BELL DIES IN IRAQ!

Gertrude Bell, the fearless British writer, traveller and archaeologist, has died at her home in the Iraqi capital of Baghdad. Often seen as a controversial figure, in her will she left £50,000 to Iraq's first major museum, which she founded before her death at the age of just fifty-seven.

Born in County Durham, England, in 1868, Bell was a leading expert on the Middle East. She rode camels with the **Bedouin** in the Arabian Desert, spoke with local leaders, and learned several languages, earning the trust and respect of those leaders along the way. For an Englishman to do this would be difficult enough – but for a woman at the time, it was quite something.

And it all put her in good stead for her later work as a spy ...

Bell was one of the first women to study at the University of Oxford. After graduating, she travelled around Europe, mastering languages including French and German before joining her uncle in Persia (the country that is now called Iran) where he was working as a British Minister in the capital city of Tehran. There, she studied Arabic and Persian, and fell in love with her uncle's secretary, a man named Henry Cadogan. Sadly, not long after they got engaged, Bell went back to England for a while, and Cadogan died of pneumonia.

Heartbroken by the news, Bell left England to travel in Italy and Switzerland, where she became a brilliant mountain climber, before heading off around the world with her brother, Maurice. In 1899, at the age of thirty-one, Gertrude Bell returned to the Middle East and headed out into the desert alone. She spent months photographing the ancient sites of Petra in Jordan and Palmyra in Syria, before returning to England. There followed another doomed romance – this time with Charles Doughty-Wylie, a married British Army officer.

After the outbreak of the First World War, in 1914, Bell took her first official job, for the international charity the Red Cross, in England. Working for the charity, she helped find missing or wounded men, and Bell was so good at it that she was later called to Cairo in Egypt, to help the British there. Except this time, the British had another job in mind for her.

Thanks to her earlier travels, Bell had learned every dialect of Arabic and Persian and, more importantly, she had met and grown to understand many of the Arab groups in the area known as the Middle East. In turn, many of them respected and trusted her. At the time, Britain and its allies were fighting against an important power in the area, known as the Ottoman Empire. Britain had long tried to gain control over the Middle East, and had succeeded at times. It was the First World War that actually enabled Britain to finally put an end to the Ottoman Empire, a move that was not welcomed by Muslims in British colonies, especially India. Britain had its own Empire to look after, as it fought to maintain influence in the world, governing a lot of it through **imperialist rule**. Keeping a hand in what was going on in the Middle East was a part of an attempt to stay in control of important areas. But in order to try to gain the upper hand, Britain had promised to help Arab groups who *were* seeking to break free from the Empire – a group led by the Hashemite-led Arabs of the Hejaz.

To enable them to do this, the British government got Bell to make use of her local friendships, so she could gather information that would help them during the war.

Bell travelled across the region, collecting information given to her by the sheikhs (Arab **scholars** and leaders), who would tell her what was going on. She wrote for *The Arab Bulletin*, a secret publication for those at the very top of the British government, explaining to them the area and its peoples. Bell also wrote for her friends and in personal diaries. In death, she left behind two volumes worth of private letters as well as poetry, non-fiction books and journalism. All of these help us understand who she was as a person, as well as a spy.

After the First World War, and the fall of the Ottoman Empire, important people from Britain gathered in Cairo for a conference, held between 12–30 March 1921. During the war, the British had made promises to Arabs, as well as Jews, and had also agreed plans with the French about how to help run the region once the Empire collapsed. The meeting in Cairo tried to find a way to honour these different promises, while ensuring Britain maintained control and influence over the area. This essentially meant the British were there to draw lines on a map, dividing up the Middle East and creating entirely new countries, while also ensuring that the European countries maintained their power. Bell was the only woman present that day.

Together with her friend, the famous explorer Lawrence of Arabia, Bell convinced the British government to make Faisal, the son of Prince Sharif Hussain of Hejaz (a kingdom that is now part of Saudi Arabia), the leader of one of these newly created countries: Iraq. This was the moment that she became the so-called 'Maker of Kings'.

It would also create lots of problems later down the line. Though the conference was supposed to lead to lasting peace, the British and French didn't always listen to local leaders or allow them a say in how things were run, and the decisions made in that room led to conflict between groups of people with competing interests. Many of these decisions were also about increasing French and British control and helping with the continuing costs of imperial rule.

This was something Gertrude herself recognized. Later that year she wrote to her mother: 'We have made an immense failure here.'

It was a failure that many believe clouded her career.

In the years leading to her unexplained death at the age of just fifty-seven, Bell remained dedicated to her adopted homeland of Iraq, and to her work. Every day she would wake before sunrise in her house on the banks of the River Tigris to write, before riding her horse to the home of her friend Haji Naji, with its extensive garden and palm groves, where they would breakfast together. She would then return to her study at around 8 a.m. to continue working.

Despite the two loves of her life, Cadogan and Doughty-Wylie (who died in battle in 1915), Bell never married. As well as her writing, Bell's legacy is in Iraq's first national museum, in Baghdad, which she founded to help protect the archaeology and incredible history of the country from loss or destruction, so that it may be enjoyed and studied by generations to come.

To some, Bell is a feminist icon, someone that girls and women might look to for inspiration. But she didn't consider herself a feminist. In fact, she actively fought against women getting the right to vote, becoming honorary secretary of the British Women's Anti-Suffrage League. Unlike the Suffragettes who fought for women to get the vote, Bell felt that women could already do whatever a man could do without the need to vote. She also believed most women weren't yet educated enough to decide how a country should be ruled ... It is yet another twist in the very complicated life of Gertrude Bell ...

# JOSEPHINE BAKER

Josephine Baker was born in St. Louis, Missouri, in the United States, in 1906. She would go on to become a truly unique performer who first caught the attention of the public when she appeared on stage in Paris, at the renowned Théâtre des Champs-Élysées. Here, and elsewhere across the world, she performed a new style of dancing called the Charleston. She soon rose to fame, and after some years became a citizen of France, the country that had embraced her. She was also a brilliant and unlikely agent for the **French Resistance** in the Second World War, where she used her fame to great effect.

Josephine was African American, and as a Black woman was deeply impacted by the racism in the

US at that time, and particularly by the violence against African-Americans during the East St. Louis Riots in 1917. She was a big fighter for the **civil rights** movement, and in the 1950s famously refused to perform at the posh Copa City nightclub in Miami Beach because African-Americans were not allowed to attend. She had already been vocal in calling out racism in the United States before she left to live in France, and it was because of the racism she faced that she chose to live in France, and fight for them during the war.

My mother's father, Basil, was a big fan of Josephine Baker. I like to think that in naming my own mother Josephine, Basil and my grandmother, Joan, were celebrating the larger-than-life dancer and singer. She was a household name when my mum was born, at the end of the Second World War. And what a woman to be named after!

As reported in the magazine *The New Yorker*, Josephine would make her entry onto the stage carried upside down (and doing the splits) on the shoulders of a giant man. As she grew famous, she could sometimes be spotted strolling through the streets of Paris with her pet, Chiquita. This was not a dog on a lead, as you might expect, but a cheetah, who sometimes appeared on stage with

Josephine wearing a collar made of diamonds. The cheetah was known to leap into the orchestra pit and terrorize the musicians.

A few years ago, I visited Château des Milandes in Dordogne, in the south of France, the house where Josephine moved after leaving Paris, and her life as a performer. The château had amazing colourful interiors and Josephine's sequinned dresses were still hanging in the wardrobe. Here is where she also raised her 'rainbow tribe', as she called them. Josephine's experience of racism had inspired her to give a home to people of all races and backgrounds, and the rainbow tribe were 12 children adopted from across the world.

I also learned, as I looked around, that Josephine Baker was a secret agent for the French Resistance, and that this house had once been a hub of espionage. It seemed incredible to think of this world-famous star being able to go undercover. But, as it turns out, her fame was the perfect disguise. As a well-known, glamorous performer, she was able to travel the world without arousing suspicion. For seven years she worked her magic as a spy fighting the Nazis.

After the war, she was awarded important medals of honour by the French military. But she was always very secretive about that time, right up until her death. As the journalist Damien Lewis writes in his book of Josephine's life: '[She] went to her grave in 1975 taking many of those secrets with her.'

Given the number of people she helped, why do you think she never spoke about these times?

Josephine doesn't lie; she improves on life.

Being a performer, and selling out shows across Paris and beyond, was no different to her second existence. She was creating a different person, an identity that people could believe in. And oh, they believed! Besides, she had always been more than one person. Maybe she didn't want to have to choose. She fought the Nazis *and* was a free spirit who loved to watch eyebrows raise as she danced. But she was never happier than when she was at home, at the château in the Dordogne, with her adopted, beloved children.

As much as it was important to her to be their mother, it was important that they were all brothers and sisters to each other. She wanted to show that people of all races and backgrounds could live happily together.

There were plenty of questions in Josephine's life. She never knew who her father was, and that not knowing left plenty of space for her imagination to run free. Depending on what sort of mood she was in, she told people he was a famous lawyer, or a tailor who made fancy outfits like the ones she wore to perform in. It was her choice to create the version of herself she wanted to tell. And her mood could change from one moment to the next.

It's a sad fact that this is one reason why Josephine and her mother struggled to have a good relationship. The other is that her mother didn't want Josephine to be an entertainer, which was considered an immoral way for a woman to live in the early 1900s. Josephine grew up in St. Louis in the United States, rummaging for coal behind Union Station to keep her home warm, and looking for scraps of food behind Soulard Market. The First World War broke out when she was only eight years old and its impact ran deep – many people went without, and many African Americans faced violence and racism from US citizens. Many fought back, though, protesting against racism and **discrimination**, and calling for equality. Having dropped out of school as a young child, Josephine grew up cleaning houses and babysitting for wealthy white families who reminded her to 'be sure not to kiss the baby'.

At the age of 13, in 1919, Josephine waitressed and danced at the Old Chauffeur's Club on Pine

Street. But if she wanted to make it big, she knew she had to get away from that town and from her mother, who had given up her own dreams of dancing to be a washerwoman.

In 1921, Josephine ran from that life (by then she'd already been married twice, at the grand ages of 13 and 15 – something that would be shocking to people now, but was more normal back then) and headed for New York City, taking a small part in a dance troupe and waiting for her time to shine. Sure enough, that time came. She dared to move to France when she was 19, desperate for the freedom that country might offer her, away from the racism she'd faced in the United States. And in Paris, Josephine danced her way to stardom.

But her greatest success came later, fighting for her adopted country in the war against the Nazis.

She was at her home in Paris when Captain Jacques Abtey, an agent at the Deuxième Bureau (one of France's intelligence agencies at the time) came knocking. Josephine was wearing a felt hat and faded trousers and searching the garden for snails to feed to her ducks. I can't imagine this is quite where the Captain expected to find a famous star, best known for preferring the finer things in life. But Josephine Baker enjoyed keeping people on their toes. She was, after all, several women at once.

The Captain was clearly on his own mission that afternoon: to decide if Josephine was to be trusted. To decide if she would really be true to France. It was September of 1939, and the Second World War had broken out. Josephine had already proven herself brave and outspoken, and vocal in calling out racism in the United States before she left to live in France.

In fact, four years earlier she had publicly declared her support for Italy's invasion of Ethiopia, which at the time she believed would help free Ethiopia's enslaved people. When the Second World War began, France and the Allied forces were fighting against Italy and its **regime**, which had sided with Nazi Germany. This was most certainly not what Josephine had signed up to when she said she'd support Italy.

But the Captain explained that suddenly her throwaway comment offered them an important opportunity. Even though Josephine no longer sided with Italy, it might help convince a friend of hers that she did. This person, as it happened, was a very important man at the Italian embassy, and he had taken rather a shine to Josephine. Maybe he would tell her things – little secrets that might help France.

In other words, said the Captain, Josephine could *pretend* to still be on the side of Italy, but really help France. When her friend in the Italian embassy told Josephine his little secrets, she would hand these secrets straight over to her French comrades. The friend didn't need to know that bit, of course.

Well, Josephine listened to what the Captain had to say and then called for champagne. She may have been American by birth, but she wanted to help France fight the Nazis, and was drawn to the challenge and the adventure of becoming a secret agent.

'France made me what I am,' she told the Captain. 'I will be grateful forever. The people of Paris have given me everything . . . You can use me as you wish.'

Then she raised a toast: 'To France.'

You might be surprised to know Josephine had a flying licence. Well, why wouldn't she have one? She owned a cheetah, after all. As Hitler's troops advanced on France, Josephine flew to the Low Countries – Belgium, the Netherlands and Luxembourg – which Germany had invaded as part of its plan to get to France. She performed for troops along the **Maginot Line** and distributed aid to refugees.

In the end, Josephine had to leave Paris, as the Nazis eventually invaded her beloved city. In June 1940, she set off for the Dordogne, in the south-west of France, with the elderly Belgian Jewish fugitives she had been giving a home to in the back of her car – helping them escape the Holocaust, and the terrible fate the Nazis had in store for them. She smuggled petrol in champagne bottles and set off for a new life in Château des Milandes, a 16th-century castle in the countryside of the Dordogne, where the lazy river swims and canoe trips were a respite from the fighting.

Not that her part in the war effort ended there. You know what they say: you can't keep a good girl down.

Instead of laying low, Captain Abtey and Josephine (they were a couple by then!) gathered together a group of resistance fighters, who stayed at the château with them. The Captain also gave Josephine a gun and a cyanide pill, full of poison, in case she was ever caught and wanted to take her own life before the Nazis could interrogate her (which would have been a brutal thing to endure). One terrifying day, German officers arrived to search the place. Josephine hid the fighters upstairs in one of the château's many rooms and played the furious lady of the manor, stomping around and shouting at the intrusion, praying none of them would be found. And they weren't.

In November 1940, she was sent on her most important mission: to deliver crucial information to the British embassy in Lisbon, Portugal. This information included intelligence about Nazi airbases and the enemy's plans to take Gibraltar – a British territory in southern Spain. In order to escape detection, Josephine pretended she was back on one of her dancing tours, and that the Captain was her tour manager. Dressed in her signature look (furs and a full face of make-up) Josephine carried her costumes in her suitcases, and the pair made their way to Lisbon by train, via Spain.

Spain, at that time, although supposed to be neutral in the war, was really part of the Axis forces, along with Germany, Italy and Japan. So this trip was highly dangerous. Tucked between the sheets of music that were in Josephine's suitcase was a file full of secrets written in invisible ink. If they had been caught . . . well, let's just say Josephine brought that cyanide pill with her, just in case.

But yet again they got away with it. The file was handed to the British embassy in Lisbon and from there into the hands of Wilfred 'Biffy' Dunderdale, an MI6 officer believed by some to be the real-life inspiration for James Bond.

It was a year later that the next verse in Josephine's life as a spy began. She was run-down from all the performing and in Morocco, living for free as the guest of Thami El Glaoui, the Pasha of Marrakech – a close friend of Josephine's and an important man in the country at the time. Here, she fell ill with a stomach problem that left her bed-bound for a year, in a hospital in Casablanca (one of Morocco's biggest cities). But Josephine's hospital bed soon became a place where people would come to visit. And these were no ordinary visitors. They'd leave top-secret information that would be collected by the Allies, also posing as friends coming to see how Josephine was. She was the hub of a spy network!

After the war ended, Josephine married her fourth husband, the conductor Jo Bouillon, and decided she wanted to have a family. She was in her forties by then, and wanted to show people that you could build a family with children from around the world – that people can live together as brother and sister, no matter the colour of their skin.

So, over the years she adopted her children from Japan, Finland, Colombia, France, Algeria, the Ivory Coast, Israel, Morocco and Venezuela. She brought them all to live with her and each other at the Château des Milandes.

It was the final chapter in a life of many parts. A life improved.

# TOOLS OF HER TRADE
## FAME

You might think that the most important thing about being a spy would be disappearing into the background. But it was Josephine Baker's fame that enabled her to hide in plain sight. When she travelled from France to Lisbon to deliver a secret file, the guards who might otherwise have searched her and questioned her reasons for travelling instead asked for her autograph! They were so star-struck that they didn't think to question whether she was secretly working as a spy, delivering intelligence to their enemies. As the expression goes, she ran them a merry dance . . .

## HISTORY DECODED

### THE HOLOCAUST

The Holocaust was the murder of six million European Jews by the Nazi German regime and its allies. It took place throughout Europe between 1933 and 1945, but the Nazi Party began to discriminate against Jews as early as the 1920s, when they bombarded Germans with anti-Jewish hate. The Nazis burned books written by Jewish authors, and eventually decided that Jewish people were not allowed to be German citizens. They attacked Jewish people, their homes, their businesses and their schools. During the Second World War, things became much, much worse and Jewish people were sent to **concentration camps** — prisons where they were forced to work, starved and murdered. This led to the Final Solution: a plan to exterminate the Jewish race. Although some Jewish people were able to escape Nazi Germany and the countries it occupied, many could not. Six million Jews were killed. During the Holocaust, Roma (Gypsies), Slavs, gay people and others also were singled out for obliteration for racial, political, and ideological reasons.

# NORTH KOREAN SPY DODGES DEATH PENALTY!

A North Korean spy gets to die another day, after her death sentence was overturned.

The woman responsible for the Korean Air Flight bombing of 1987 was originally arrested in Bahrain following the bombing, in which 115 people were killed. Kim Hyon-Hui was then sent to South Korea for trial, where she was sentenced to death.

Now the spy, who started her career as an actress and starred in North Korea's first colour film, has had her death penalty lifted by South Korean President, Roh Tae-woo. The president claimed she had been brainwashed by the North Korean government.

Korea was divided into two countries – North Korea and South Korea – after the Second World War, and remains this way today. Back then, the South was occupied by the US and the North by the Soviet Union. The North is still a communist state today, and it is a brutal, repressive, secretive regime. The South is relatively free.

Hyon-Hui was born in North Korea. She studied Japanese at university before being recruited as a spy, and given the new name Ok Hwa.

According to what she told South Korean police after her arrest, she was trained in martial arts and learned to speak Japanese and Cantonese at a compound outside the North Korean capital of Pyongyang. Things that might seem everyday to many of us, like credit cards, didn't exist in North Korea. As part of her training, Hyon-Hui was taught how to use a bank card and how to go shopping, so that when

she was sent abroad she could blend in and not seem suspicious.

Hyon-Hui spent six years learning the tools of spycraft. During this time, she claimed that she was told South Korea was a terrible place, controlled by the United States, where people were greedy and uncaring of others, and that its government was corrupt.

In 1987, Hyon-Hui was given a fake passport in the name of Mayumi Hachiya and sent on a mission with her partner in crime – an older man – to bomb flight KAL 858. A flight that would have had many South Korean passengers on board. She was told that, after she had done this, she could return to her family and would no longer have to work for the North Korean government.

When the day came, Hyon-Hui and her partner got on the Korean Airlines plane in Baghdad in Iraq. She placed the bomb, hidden in a suitcase, in the locker above their seat. The plane was due to stop in Abu Dhabi, a city in the United Arab Emirates, to fill up with fuel. When the passengers got off, Hyon-Hui and her partner left the airport.

Hours later, when the plane was back in the air, flying over the Andaman Sea, the bomb went off and killed all 115 people on board.

But the bombers didn't get away with it. The police who were investigating became suspicious when they realized the pair hadn't returned to the plane. And when the police looked again at their passports, they saw that they were fake.

The two agents were tracked down in Bahrain, an island country in West Asia, and caught. Hyon-Hui was taken by South Korean agents to its capital, Seoul. The agents wanted her to face justice in South Korea, and wanted to make sure she could see that the country she had been taught to fear wasn't corrupt or riddled with poverty, like the North Korean **propaganda** had taught her.

Kim Hyon-Hui then said she regretted the terrible crime she had committed, and admitted to everything she'd done. By confessing that North Korea was behind the attack, she was also showing South Korea how dangerous the North could be to them.

She was originally sentenced to death, but a year later she has been pardoned, and will spend the rest of her days in a secret location, with a new identity, to protect her from anyone out for revenge.

In her confession she said that the orders to bomb the plane had come directly from North Korean leader, Kim Il-sung – supposedly in a handwritten note.

# FAMOUS WOMEN YOU DIDN'T KNOW WERE SPIES!

### AUDREY HEPBURN

The Hollywood actress best known for her part in *Breakfast at Tiffany's* was a very private person.

What we do know is that she was born in Belgium and spent her early childhood there, as well as in England and Holland. Her mother was Dutch, and her father was English, and both her parents initially supported fascism (but later changed their minds). During the war Hepburn helped to raise money for the Dutch Resistance, taking part in illegal dance performances to raise cash.

These evenings were called black evenings, because the windows were blacked out in order to protect the secrecy of the event. Audiences were forbidden from clapping at the end of the dance for the same reason.

Hepburn might also have delivered a Resistance newspaper by bicycle, hiding copies in her woollen socks.

## MARLENE DIETRICH

You may know the performer Marlene Dietrich for her sultry singing. But did you also know the German-born star was a spy? Marlene became a United States citizen after refusing Hitler's order to return to Germany when war broke out.

Instead, she risked her own safety to entertain American troops on the front lines, where the army are closest to their enemy and therefore vulnerable to attack. Then, in 1944, she was approached by the US secret agency, the OSS, to work for them.

In a case of musical subterfuge, Dietrich was asked to record songs that would be broadcast, by radio, to German troops. But she was also asked to sing the German lyrics in such a way that it would lower the mood of the German troops and encourage the soldiers to change sides – which she did. After the war, her efforts were rewarded when she received the Medal of Freedom, America's highest civilian honour.

## JULIA CHILD

Julia Child, the famous American cook, was another well-known person with a double life as an agent for the OSS. And she operated during the same period as Marlene Dietrich. Child had always wanted to join the US Army, but was told that at six feet two inches, she was too tall!

Her height didn't stop her joining the US secret intelligence services, though – firstly as a secretary and then helping develop a shark repellent, so that sharks would no longer accidentally trigger underwater bombs meant for enemy ships. The repellent is still used today. When asked about her time with the service, Child said, 'I was not a spy, only a lowly file clerk.' But she received an Emblem of Meritorious Civilian Service for her efforts, so take that with a pinch of salt . . .

# KRYSTYNA SKARBEK (OR CHRISTINE GRANVILLE)

When those who knew Krystyna Skarbek talk about her, they tend to describe her as incredibly brave. The great spymaster Vera Atkins was more specific. She said that Skarbek was 'very brave, very attractive, but a loner and a law unto herself'. I love this idea of a daring, gorgeous rule-breaker, skiing at great speed over the snow-capped mountains, crossing frontiers in order to deliver intelligence.

I'm sure this is how she would want to be remembered. Rather than through the miserable and tragic circumstances of her death.

Krystyna Skarbek – or Christine Granville, as she later became – was born on 1 May 1908 in Warsaw, Poland. An agent of the British Special Operations Executive during the Second World War, her work was dangerous, and might not always have felt as glamorous as it sounds. But as the longest-serving of Britain's female agents in the SOE, her life does read like something from a film.

Krystyna was the daughter of a Polish count and her mother came from a line of Jewish bankers. She was a brilliant skier who grew up on a grand country estate and spent much of her childhood riding horses and learning to use guns and knives – the perfect preparation for a future secret agent – before a brief first marriage to a businessman named Gustaw Gettlich. She met her second husband, Jerzy Giżycki, a Polish **diplomat** (and, like her father, also a count), on the ski slopes and they married not long before the outbreak of the Second World War.

The couple were on holiday when Germany invaded Poland and the war broke out. Immediately, they sailed to London, and Krystyna offered to work for the British government. As a Pole, she felt this was the best possible way for her to fight against Nazi Germany, which was an enemy of both Poland and Britain.

When Krystyna and her husband arrived in London, in October 1939, no one paid her much attention. But a well-connected journalist persuaded the British Secret Intelligence Service (MI6) to take note of this fearless, brilliant woman.

With the journalist's help, she met an intelligence officer named George Taylor and presented him with a mad-cap plan to go to Hungary and from there travel over the mountains to Poland – by skis! In Poland she would recruit volunteers to fight the Germans, help people escape, smuggle weapons and get hold of useful information. Taylor agreed to the plan.

In his report of the meeting, Taylor wrote: 'She is a flaming Polish patriot, an expert skier and great adventuress. I really believe we have a PRIZE.' And he wasn't wrong.

It was on her first spy mission, in Budapest, Hungary, in 1940 that Krystyna properly met the man who would become the true love of her life (having left her second husband behind). Andrzej Kowerski was a Polish army officer and secret agent. They had met briefly as children and were reunited while working together for the SOE. Under the direction of MI6, the couple were in charge of keeping a watch on the roads, railways and rivers that formed the borders between Romania and Germany. Then, in January 1941, Krystyna and Kowerski were arrested by the Gestapo in Hungary. As we will see, Krystyna used all her bravery and wits to get out of that very dangerous situation . . .

Tragically, after the war, and once her life as a spy had come to an end, Krystyna (by then a British citizen, going by the name of Christine) was stabbed to death in London. Her murderer was a man named Dennis George Muldowney, who had become obsessed with Krystyna after they worked together on a cruise ship. It seems so sad that Krystyna survived so much danger in her life, and was killed in a terrible, pointless act.

There is a plaque to her memory on the house in Kensington where she lived for the final three years of her life. Before her death in 1952, she had been awarded a George Medal and an OBE by the British, and a Croix de Guerre by the French – all in recognition of her bravery.

In a way, Krystyna has been training to be a spy all her life. From her childhood, she knew how to use a knife and a gun – which is the type of early training you get growing up rich and largely left to your own devices on a big country estate. She also knew how to get from one place to another by skis, a method of travel unlikely to raise suspicion.

If there is such thing as heaven, then for Krystyna it was the snow-capped peaks with the sun reflecting on the surface as she weaved her way back and forth down the slopes, transporting intelligence and escapees. (At one point she was even smuggling secrets on **microfilm**, slipped inside her gloves!)

To the rest of the world, she must have appeared like a young woman enjoying her freedom. But in reality, that freedom meant nothing to her while others were suffering at the hands of the Germans. Besides, she didn't want a life spent idly drifting across gentle hills admiring the view. She wanted adventure. She wanted to forge her own path, off the beaten track.

Those days and nights were long and dangerous, but Krystyna relished the challenge, secretly transporting weapons and cash (and even sometimes explosives) across borders to help resistance fighters against the Nazis.

It was on her first mission that she met Andrzej Kowerski again: her true love. Andrzej's father would sometimes bring him to Krystyna's house, to play with her, while the grown-ups chatted about farming. By the time they met again, years later, Andrzej was a Polish army officer.

They clicked right away.

On the borders between Romania and Germany, they kept an eye on Nazi traffic, providing the British secret service with information about oil moving from Romania's oilfields to Germany's factories. A supply of oil was important to the Nazis, for everything from heating houses to working their weapons. If the British knew when and where the transport carrying the oil would turn up, they could try to stop it in its tracks.

But it was in Budapest where they really showed the enemy what they were made of. This was after they were taken by the Hungarian police and imprisoned and questioned by the Gestapo.

Sometimes Krystyna wakes up in a cold sweat remembering the moment they were arrested, how her heart galloped in her chest as they were led towards their interrogation. Strange to think that a disease like tuberculosis is the thing that saved them. After two days of their questioning, Krystyna had the bright idea of biting her tongue so hard that she spat out blood. She claimed that this was coming up from her lungs, because of the TB she was sick with. They fell for it, letting the pair go in the belief that they were infected with a deadly and highly contagious disease!

With the help of the British ambassador, Owen O'Malley, and his wife, Ann, they escaped Hungary. Krystyna was smuggled out of the country and into Yugoslavia in the boot of O'Malley's car, and Andrzej drove separately across the border. Thanks to O'Malley and their new British passports, Andrzej became Andrew Kennedy, and Krystyna became Christine Granville.

With that name, which she kept for the rest of her life, Krystyna undertook her greatest mission yet.

It was July 1944. Krystyna always admitted she was terrible at using a gun and radios, but loved parachuting. And so she was parachuted into France to act as a **courier**, working as second-in-command to Francis Cammaerts, code name 'Roger'. Francis had been a **conscientious objector** in the beginning, and refused to fight. But by the time Krystyna met him, code name Roger was going up against the Germans in the Vercors Plateau (a mountain range in southern France) and by the summer of 1944 he had put together a force of more than 10,000 people willing to work against the Nazi occupiers.

Some people assumed that after the Allied landings in Normandy (**D-Day**), the Germans would focus on northern France. But instead they attacked Vercours – and they were ruthless. Even so, Krystyna and her team continued to organize their fighters to tackle German soldiers, to weaken them before a big attack by the Allies on 15 August. This was called Operation Dragoon.

Krystyna's part in preparing for the operation involved her and Roger hiking for 70 miles in just 24 hours to get messages to the resistance fighters. Seventy miles in 24 hours means the exhausting task of walking three miles an hour without stopping. You might think Krystyna would be relieved that part of her life was over, but that's probably untrue. She longed for adventure.

The operation succeeded. After four weeks and two days of fighting, German forces were forced to retreat from most of southern France.

The final stage of Krystyna's career as a spy was perhaps the most impressive (if that is how we judge these things). Thinking about her quiet life in London, Krystyna might find it difficult to believe she was the same person who managed to tame a German Alsatian dog that had been trained to kill, and make it become loyal to her instead (the dog wouldn't leave Krystyna's side!). Or the same woman who managed to secure the release of Roger and two other agents from the clutches of the German secret police . . .

It was August 1944 and already it was clear the Allies were on their way to winning the war. Krystyna knew that there was a price on her head by then – that the Germans were offering to pay anyone who could arrest or kill her. She couldn't risk being recognized. But nor could she leave

Roger and two other men, who were due to be executed that afternoon.

This particular summer, in 1944, it was Roger's job to recruit, arm and train the resistance fighters over a large area in France. He was careful, but not careful enough, and was soon arrested by the Gestapo.

Krystyna could hardly try to break into the cell where her commander was being held, unnoticed. Instead, she argued with the Germans in charge and, in a fit of temper, declared that she was the niece of General Montgomery – then commander of the Allied forces! – and, as the Allies were about to win the war, she had been ordered to take the captives home. If they didn't release her men at once, Krystyna said, then she would make sure there would be terrible trouble for them once the Allies were in control.

Her palms must have been sweating as she tried to look like she was in charge. Somehow, they didn't notice that Krystyna was playing pretend, and her bravado paid off. The strength it must have taken to keep the smile off her face as she walked out of that room, knowing that her commander and their men would soon be safely at her side . . .

Here in London, now that the war is over, Krystyna finds herself trying to get used to normal life. She has taken on simple jobs. She even worked for a time as a steward on a cruise ship, where she briefly had a relationship with a man called Dennis. She hoped that being at sea might bring her something like the sense of adventure she had known and been inspired by during the war. But the time on the ship hasn't filled the hole left behind.

The relationship with Dennis isn't anything serious, even if he seemed to think it was something more than it was. From her room on the first floor of the Shellbourne Hotel, sometimes, at night, Krystyna thinks she can see Dennis outside, watching her. Perhaps she is being paranoid after the years spent hiding in the shadows.

As we know, tragically, Krystyna was right to trust her instincts . . .

# TOOLS OF HER TRADE
## SKIS

Krystyna Skarbek had a number of tools in her kitbag. Like the other women we've met so far, these included being able to speak many languages, quick wits and bravery. But her excellent skiing abilities meant that she could travel across borders, undetected, at a time when the Axis forces had eyes everywhere. After all, who would suspect a beautiful young woman, enjoying a day skiing on the mountains, of secretly helping escapees and carrying explosives?

## HISTORY DECODED

### GESTAPO

'Gestapo' means 'Secret State Police'.
In Nazi Germany, it was ruthless about
dealing with anyone who disagreed
with Nazi beliefs, attacking everyone
from priests and students to teachers,
soldiers and members of trade unions.
The Gestapo might have been small, but
it was effective because its officers
encouraged people to spy and inform on
one another in order to keep control.
Many died at the hands of the Gestapo.

# OBITUARY:
# IRA SPY AND PRISON-BREAK REPUBLICAN DIES AGED 88

An Irish Republican spy who escaped prison twice has died at the age of 88. The youngest of seven children, Eithne Coyle was born Annie Coyle on 3 January 1897 in Killult, a village on the north tip of Ireland, in County Donegal.

In 1917, at the age of twenty, Eithne Coyle joined Cumann na mBan, an Irish republican women's paramilitary organization. That is, a group of rebels who organize themselves like an army. In this case, the rebels were fighting for Irish independence from Britain. Eithne raised money for Cumann na mBan and campaigned against conscription (when people are forced to join the armed forces).

In 1919, the Irish Republican Army (IRA) formed to fight against British rule in Ireland, and the War of Independence broke out. Eithne Coyle joined the fight. The IRA's enemies were the Irish loyalists (known as Unionists), who wanted Ireland to remain part of Great Britain.

It was a bloody war. In two years of fighting, 1,400 people

died. Around 600 of those were members of the British security forces, while more than 700 were members of the IRA or ordinary people simply living their lives.

While Coyle was fighting, her home was raided and its contents burned by the Irish police force who supported the Unionists and were looking for evidence that she was part of the rebel group. On 1 January 1921, she was arrested and found guilty of keeping documents that encouraged people to rise up against those in charge. Coyle was imprisoned in different areas of Ireland – Roscommon, Athlone and Mountjoy. While in these jails, she planned her escape,

and how she would continue her fight once she was free.

In October 1921, Eithne and three other women broke out of Mountjoy Jail with the aid of prison wardens, who helped the prisoners climb over the prison wall. The women escaped in cars driven by republicans, who were waiting outside, and were given shelter in Dublin, Kilcullen, and finally at Ducketts Grove in Carlow. When a truce was declared at the end of the war and fighting stopped, Eithne Coyle returned to Donegal.

But peace didn't last long. The Irish War of Independence had ended with 26 counties becoming the Irish Free State, and the six northeastern counties becoming Northern Ireland (and remaining a part of the UK). This was called the partition of Ireland. But while Unionists in the North wanted to remain part of the UK, Republicans in Northern Ireland did not. This led to over 30 years of violent conflict in the North, where the IRA fought to remove the British presence from Northern Ireland and to unite the 32 counties.

Eithne Coyle travelled to Dublin to continue to fight for true independence from Britain, working as a volunteer carrying weapons and secret messages back and forth between members of her rebel group. Again, she was arrested and locked up in Mountjoy Jail and released in 1923 following a ceasefire. This happened when IRA leaders ordered its forces to stand down and stop fighting on 30 April 1923.

But Eithne Coyle never quit her quest for Irish independence.

Three years later she became President of Cumann na mBan, the rebel group that she had first joined at the age of 20. The next time she was arrested, it was for pulling down British flags flying on O'Connell Street in the centre of Dublin.

Eithne had one son and one daughter with her husband, Bernard O'Donnell, who died in February 1968. While the IRA has been condemned for being a terrorist group, Eithne's commitment to its cause remained firm until her death.

# NOOR INAYAT KHAN

Noor Inayat Khan's story is very moving, but it is also a tale of an unlikely spy who had total certainty in what she was doing. Noor was born in Moscow in 1914, and died in Dachau concentration camp in September 1944, at the age of thirty.

Noor's Indian father, Inayat Rehmat Khan (known to some as Hazrat Inayat Khan), was descended from royalty. He was a pacificist, meaning he was opposed to all violence and war. Inayat was also a professor of music and taught the traditions of Sufism, a branch of Islam that celebrates devotion through music and meditation. He met Noor's American mother in the United States, where he was teaching music. She was pregnant when Noor's father was invited to Moscow for a concert, and it was there, in Russia, that Noor was born.

This was 1914 and, shortly after, when the First World War broke out, the family moved to London and then on to Paris, where Noor learned to speak fluent French. Tragically, when Noor was 13 her father died, and it was left to Noor to look after her younger brothers and sisters. She later studied child psychology at the Sorbonne, a university in Paris, and music at the Paris Conservatory. From childhood she wrote poetry and stories, which were published in children's magazines and on French radio.

My favourite part of Noor's story is when British officers questioned Noor about her loyalty to Britain. Noor was 28 years old now, living in London, and proud of her Indian heritage. While Noor was with the **Women's Auxiliary Air Force** during the Second World War, a lot of people in India were asking for British rule of the country to come to an end (see HISTORY DECODED on page 141). And Mahatma Gandhi was calling on the British to 'quit India' – meaning they should leave the country and return it back to Indian rule, so it could be independent (see page 143).

Noor was called for an interview by the RAF, possibly for a promotion, but the British officers who questioned Noor weren't sure whether they could trust her. They asked her if she believed in Indian independence, and if so, would that prevent her from being able to fight for Britain?

According to Noor's biographer, Shrabani Basu, who spent years reading Noor's papers and interviewing her family, Noor replied very honestly. Of course she wanted the British out of India, she said, and yes, she believed in Indian independence. But she had to prioritize. She told them that, at this time, the most important issue was to win the war in Europe and beat the Nazis – an opinion also held by several Indian leaders at the time. After the war was won, she would believe in Indian independence again.

This says so much about Noor's spirit, showing her determination and an ability to believe in what is right – both Indian independence and defeating the Nazis. Today, Noor is recognized as a national hero and is the only agent of South Asian descent to have been given a British award called the George Cross, which honours heroism and which she was awarded after her death.

Noor knew her decision to put her life on the line as a spy would upset her mother. But she believed that beating the Nazis was more important than protecting her own family.

What do you think of this choice?

Noor's code name was Madeleine, her alias Jeanne-Marie Rennier. She taught herself to become Jeanne-Marie, practising her signature again and again during her training at various country homes across England. Noor had always committed herself to any task at school, and this was no different.

A typical training day in the life of Noor, agent of the SOE, might go something like this . . .

Morning: learn Morse code, followed by training on how to scramble over rooftops and attach secret radio transmitters to the chimney stacks of buildings without being seen.

Afternoon: a lesson in how to travel on a fake passport, or pass messages using a dead drop (which involves leaving an item in a secret location).

Night-time: practise the curve of the letters of her new name until it comes naturally:

*Jeanne-Marie Rennier*

Noor had to leave her past behind the moment she was selected as a field agent for the Secret Operations Executive. Until the day, almost a year ago, when she came home to her flat and found the German secret police waiting for her.

Here in Dachau, the concentration camp where she is being held, she is neither Madeleine nor Noor. She left any trace of her fake identity, and what she had done as Madeleine, the moment she was arrested. Despite the torture and their interrogations over the months, she has given them nothing. Not even her real name.

When they kill Noor for being a British agent in the French Resistance, as they soon will, they will take away her body. But in her mind, she has already left their hateful shackles, and is back with her mother and father in the house in Paris. In her imagination, her mother is dressed in one of her beautiful saris, smiling proudly as she and her siblings play music. When she closes her eyes, she can feel the strings of the harp against her fingers and hear the notes of the piano and violin as her brother and sister play alongside.

Noor was an unlikely spy. She was always quiet – 'a dreamer' according to her teachers. But dreaming to Noor was a way of making sense of the world, and of other people. Dreaming allowed her to write stories and to compose music. Dreaming wasn't her weakness, it was her strength. Right now, dreams are what allow Noor to imagine herself somewhere else, outside of her prison cell.

Sometimes she thinks back to 1939, the year the war broke out, and the year Noor's book *Twenty Jataka Tales* was published in London. She hopes her mother will read the book, and hear her through its words and in those stories she has written about the twenty lives of Buddha. She is so proud to have this legacy, and prays it will bring her mother some comfort.

It was Noor's brother, Vilayat, who inspired her to help the war effort; in Noor's case by joining the Women's Auxiliary Air Force (part of the Royal Air Force during the war). But she doesn't blame him for what has happened. Noor knew when she joined that her mother would worry, but knew also that she had to sign up to fight. She hopes her father would have respected her choice. The Nazis and their allies were destroying the world, and if she could do anything to help stop them, she was duty-bound to do it.

She worked hard. Maybe more so because she wanted to prove that a woman could do the job of any man, and do it well. And it paid off.

One day she was called into a meeting. When she arrived, there was just one man sitting at the table. He asked Noor some questions and then, just like that, she was invited to join the Special Operations Executive, to work in F section. This section was responsible for many of SOE's activities in France, after the country fell to the Nazis.

During her time in the Air Force, Noor had proven herself a fast learner and good at Morse code. Plus, she was fluent in French. As an SOE agent, she would be sent to occupied Paris as a wireless operator, which would allow London to talk to their agents in France. She'd provide the Allies with information on German defences (and how they could break them), and carry out acts of sabotage against the Germans. If she was caught, she would be shot.

Would Noor do it? Of course she would; she didn't hesitate.

Noor knew her mother would be heartbroken at the thought of her daughter putting her life at risk. Especially given that, as a pacifist, her father had been so against war of any kind. But she felt the war was more important than her feelings, or her safety. So she 'disappeared', and not one of her family or friends knew the truth of where she was going. She couldn't risk one of them accidentally giving away her new secret life.

One morning, they woke up and Noor had simply gone.

Noor was the first woman ever to be sent to occupied France in the role of wireless operator. What an honour that was for her, but also what a responsibility! Before Noor, other women in the SOE had only been sent to France as couriers, not tasked with actually sending information back to the bosses using a radio. She had to prove herself, and prove that she would not let the Allies down.

For three months, Noor carried a suitcase radio, using it to send her reports back to France. It looked just like a regular rectangle suitcase from the outside, but with radio machinery inside. It weighed 30 lb, which was more than a quarter of Noor's own weight! Without any help, she kept communications between London and occupied Paris going – sharing vital information while German soldiers manned the streets. The day Noor was arrested by the Gestapo she had already helped thirty British airmen avoid being caught by the Nazis.

It nearly ended so differently.

With Noor's mission nearly over, she was preparing to return home to her mother and her siblings at their house in London. One evening, she strode up the steps to her Paris apartment and let herself in – planning, in her head, what she would do when the family were all together again. Then, as she turned on the light, she saw the Gestapo officer waiting for her inside.

She fought him. She bit the man as he tried to arrest her, kicking him so hard that he had to call in back-up to bundle her into the car. By the time they got Noor to 84 Avenue Foch – the main Gestapo headquarters in the city – she had decided she wouldn't give them a single piece of information. And she didn't. Despite the torture and the beating, she never said a word. Except one, to herself: *Liberté*. Freedom. Noor would never give up trying to be free.

Twice she tried to escape, and once nearly succeeded. By using Morse code, tapping the walls of their cells, Noor and her fellow prisoners talked to each other through the prison walls and planned their bid for freedom. That night, three of them managed to get out of their cells, and on to the roofs of the headquarters. Noor will never forget that taste of liberty ... or the sense of dread she felt as the sound of the sirens went off.

It is bitter irony that the British Royal Air Force – the same RAF where Noor had first served – had started a bombing raid on the city, not knowing that Noor and her fellow prisoners were in the middle of their escape. When the alarms went off, the prison guards did their usual checks on the prisoners and found that they were missing from their cells.

They were rounded up. Because of Noor's attempt to escape she was then labelled a 'highly dangerous' prisoner. The Gestapo moved her from the headquarters to Pforzheim prison, on the edge of the Black Forest in Germany. For ten months they kept her there, shackled in chains and foot irons, kept away from other prisoners. Still Noor never revealed a thing about any of the people she worked with, or for. When she was at her lowest, it was thoughts of her family that comforted her.

Noor was purposefully only given food when the prison corridor was empty, so that she had no chance to even see another prisoner. But she managed to communicate with her fellow women inmates by scratching messages on to the bowls in which they gave the prisoners their food. The bowls were then passed between the rooms by the guards, who remained oblivious. The prisoners started sending messages back and forth in this way, sharing phrases like 'Vive la France' and words of encouragement.

They also shared their addresses, scratching them on to the metal bowls along with the message. And through the songs they sang Noor and her fellow prisoners imagined how they would celebrate when they were free.

Then, after ten months, some of the prisoners, including Noor, were sent from that prison to Dachau, not knowing what would become of them. During the journey, they were given sausages and allowed to speak English to one another. They blinked in wonder as they watched the mountains of south Germany pass by. They were told they would be doing farming work when they arrived, and even though Noor realized that she was foolish to believe this, hope is a powerful emotion.

The moment they saw the camp, they knew they had been lied to.

These might be her final hours but, until the last, Noor stayed a true Inayat Khan, and true to her beliefs – to the values her parents taught her. More than anything, Noor wants her mother not to dwell on how she'll die – but instead, to remember how she lived.

# TOOLS OF HER TRADE
## RADIO OPERATOR

Noor was bilingual, speaking both English and French. This made her the perfect person to go undercover in occupied Paris as an ordinary citizen, regularly dying her hair and changing her appearance. But while most women who spied for SOE worked as couriers, passing information back and forth between France and Britain, Noor was a radio operator. This meant that as well as gathering information, it fell to her to assemble and place secret radio equipment. This had to be kept hidden when not in use (sometimes in a suitcase), and when she wanted to send or receive a message, she had to put up an aerial, disguising it as best she could. Without getting caught, Noor had to smuggle her equipment into Paris, then climb onto rooftops to assemble the radio transmitter, where it would get a signal, before using the radio to talk to her spymaster bosses. It was skilled and dangerous work, and Noor did it brilliantly.

At one point she was stopped by German police on the Paris Metro (the city's underground train system) and asked what was inside her suitcase. When the police opened it and saw the machinery,

Noor told them it was used for cinematography (the equipment used to show films in the cinema) and they were so embarrassed for not knowing what she was talking about they let her go. At that time, a polite and petite young woman must not have looked to them like an obvious candidate for a spy. In the end, Noor was caught only because one of her fellow spy's sisters handed her in, in return for money. The Gestapo later said they would have paid ten times the amount in order to catch Noor. She was that brilliant a radio operator, and a brave young woman to the end.

## HISTORY DECODED

### INDIAN INDEPENDENCE

The Indian Independence Bill was a hard fight for historic freedom. By the time the bill passed, in 1947, India had been under some form of British rule for nearly two centuries.

As far back as the 1600s, British traders had visited India to buy things

like tea and spices and herbs. In 1757,
the East India Company, a powerful
trading company run by the British, had
taken control in eastern India, and
went on to take over most of the rest
of the country through military might.
As the company grew richer, India grew
poorer. Something drastic needed to be
done. The British government's solution
was to rule over India completely
and make India a British colony. By
1858, India — which then also included
what is now Pakistan and Bangladesh —
officially became part of the British
Crown. In other words, Britain decided
to rule the country. But although the
British Raj, as the new British-run
government was known, claimed to have
improved the country in many ways,
in reality India was no better off.
This was something Britain had been
doing around the world, very often
exploiting the people and resources of
the countries it claimed to rule, often
through violence and oppression.

Britain's rule of India had also often been unfair and violent, and led to recurrent famines and poverty. Some Indian leaders felt the way to take the country back was to fight the British and its supporters in India. Others wanted to do so by peaceful means. None more famously than the pacifist Indian lawyer and politician Mahatma Gandhi, who believed he could get his message across without violence.

Finally, peaceful protests led by Mahatma Gandhi, Jawaharlal Nehru and others — along with other calls for freedom, and many protest movements — resulted in the Indian Independence Bill. Against Gandhi's wishes, this divided British India into the independent nations of India and Pakistan — a process called Partition. The British decided that India and Pakistan should be divided into two free, independent countries, along religious lines. But when the new borders were announced, 15 million people suddenly became religious minorities on either side of the border, and tried to cross to the other side. Fierce fighting erupted. Hundreds of thousands were killed, many in Punjab and Bengal, regions that border West and East India, and it's estimated that 1 million people died (though the number may be higher). Since 1947, there have been several wars between India and Pakistan.

# READ ALL ABOUT IT

*24 JUNE 2005*

# SOE'S VERA ATKINS DEVOTED HER LIFE TO SEARCHING FOR 100 MISSING AGENTS!

Vera Atkins was a Special Operations Executive agent working in France during the Second World War. Much has been written about her time in F section – first as assistant to its leader, Maurice Buckmaster, and later as an intelligence officer. But five years after her death in 2000, a new book by journalist Sarah Helm tells another chapter in her story . . .

It celebrates the effort Atkins made to find out what happened to more than a hundred SOE agents, who were still missing when the agency was closed down after the war ended.

Atkins worked tirelessly to find out what had happened to the agents, which included 14 women, 12 of whom she had personally escorted to the airfield before they left for their mission in France. She was able to find out what had happened to every single agent, except one.

As part of her determined investigations, Atkins also interviewed fellow prisoners and prison guards from the agents' time in captivity in occupied France and Germany. Atkins tried to piece together the prisoners' final moments, returning to the places where they would have been, and even in some cases reading notes they had managed to scratch onto the walls of their cells. She was able to bring together details that offer some sense of closure and comfort for the agents' families and loved ones. One of the agents whose final months Vera Atkins traced included Noor Inayat Khan. It wasn't until Vera Atkins delivered her discovery to Noor's mother and siblings that they knew what had happened to her.

# EDITH TUDOR-HART

I've told you how I first learned about photographer and Soviet recruiter Edith Tudor-Hart, who was responsible for my grandfather's life as a double agent. Though I don't agree with everything she did, her story breaks my heart. Not least because of how, in the end, she was separated from her son.

Edith was born in Vienna, Austria, on 28 August 1908 and died in Brighton, England, in 1973.

As a spy, she gave her all to what she believed in. But she also gave everything she could to her only child, Tommy, taking him to see the best doctors of the time, who are still famous today – Anna Freud and Donald Winnicott. But no one could help him.

We don't know exactly what was wrong with Tommy but today he might have been diagnosed as having **schizophrenia**, a long-term mental health condition. He ended up in a psychiatric hospital in Scotland, far from Edith, who by the end of her life was left penniless and running an antique shop in Brighton. Years later I would pass the shop every day as a student, when I was at university in the city. I love the idea that, without knowing it at the time, I was walking the same pavements that Edith had walked decades earlier.

Edith was Jewish, and grew up in a working-class part of Vienna in the shadow of the First World War. Her father, Wilhelm, and his brother, Philipp, ran the first socialist bookshop in the city. Brüder Suschitzky was its name. They published and sold books about all sorts of ideas that were quite unusual and radical at the time – books about the rights of the working classes and books that were feminist, about the rights of women – until they were seized and burned by the police.

Tragically, weeks after Edith moved to London in 1934, her father took his own life. He, like many Jews in Austria at the time, was scared of what would become of him. Jewish people were terrified by the rise of Hitler in Germany, and Nazism, which was spreading across Europe. Books by Jewish authors were burnt and Jewish businesses boycotted, and the first concentration camp had been built a year earlier. Suddenly the world felt very dangerous and threatening.

Edith loved children. At the age of 16 she first travelled from Vienna to London, alone, to train under the famous teacher Maria Montessori, and then she returned to Austria to work in a nursery in Vienna. She then went to Germany, to attend the modernist Bauhaus school to learn photography.

Modernists believed in the power of the future, rather than always looking to the past. This reflects how Edith viewed the ideas of communism and how she believed those ideas could change the world.

By the time she arrived at the Bauhaus in 1928, aged 20, Edith was already a member of the Communist Party and working for the NKVD, the Soviet secret police. And to the day she died, she never gave up her belief in communism.

The question Edith asked herself at the end of her life was: did she do enough?

The short answer is that she believed she did what she could. She had no regrets about her choices. It was tough being a single mother and a secret agent, all the while trying to make enough money as a photographer to put food on the table. But it was also a privilege.

When she looked back at her life, she saw herself as several people at once. Being Tommy's mother never got in the way of her commitment to the ideas she believed in. And she truly believed. If anything, Tommy reminded her of the importance of creating a world that she could have hope in.

But it was strange for Edith to think of Tommy there in Scotland, and her without the money to visit him. To hold his hand, as a mother should.

Perhaps she blamed Kim Philby for allowing himself to be discovered as a double agent for the Soviets, leaving her in the firing line. But to lay blame is a dangerous path. And she was no fool. Her life was a series of choices, with dangerous consequences, and she stood by each of them. If you asked her why she did what she did – why she chose to give her life to the communist cause – she told you that she was a soldier. That she heard the call of duty and answered.

But that's only part of the story. The other truth is that there are no winners in war, even silent wars like the one Edith fought.

Kim Philby, Guy Burgess, Donald Maclean and the rest of those men were all exposed. But for Edith, despite all those years of being followed, of her post being intercepted and read, and her phone calls listened in on – they still couldn't prove a thing. In the end, though, they made it impossible for Edith to work in London, which meant she never had enough money to visit Tommy at the hospital in Aberdeen. They wanted to keep Edith from her son, to break her down so she'd confess everything she knew about the Cambridge Five. This was after Kim Philby was caught, exposed as the 'Third Man', and he escaped to Moscow. They had found a copy of the photograph she'd taken of him, decades earlier, proving that she'd known him. They wanted to use that against her, to frighten her into giving him up. But they couldn't.

And when they couldn't make Edith talk, they tried to break her spirit. But she never fell apart completely.

After Tommy went away and Edith was hounded out of London, she opened a little antique shop on Bond Street in Brighton. Tommy would have loved it there, with the beach and the pier. Sometimes she smiled to herself as she walked along the seafront, imagining how she must look to the outside world: just a little old lady, no threat to anyone. It's the way it always was. Even when they were following her, night and day, as she passed British secrets to her Russian handler, the British government could never quite believe that she was a real danger to them. She was just a poor woman from a different country, with no real friends and no access to the rings of power that run the world. And she was a single mother. So she was nothing to be frightened of, surely.

How much they didn't know . . .

In 1938, Tommy was just two years old, and Edith was living in London. Tommy's father and Edith had already broken up and she was working as a photographer in a studio. Tommy was nestled in the buggy beside her when she bought the camera she used to photograph secret documents – documents that were handed to her through a chain of people who chose to betray Britain.

That chain started with Percy Glading, a communist who worked at the Royal Arsenal in Woolwich. Known as the Secret City, it was where weapons were designed and built for war. Percy had got hold of secret plans to do with the development of some of these weapons and gave these to his secretary, Olga Gray.

Olga was a communist too – or so Edith thought – and was next in the chain. She had been trusted by Percy to be in charge of a safe house in London where the Communist Party of Great Britain had their meetings.

That's where Edith came in. She met Olga at the safe house, and photographed the plans to hand over to Arnold Deutsch, her Soviet handler.

The final link in the chain, Arnold would then give the photographs to his Soviet spymasters, and so hand over information of huge importance.

Little did Percy know that Olga was telling everything to her controllers at MI5. Olga was a double agent. She was good – Edith never suspected a thing. Perhaps she was as naive as they were, believing that a mere secretary could never pose a threat.

Thanks to Olga, Percy was arrested in 1938 for stealing those secrets and later sentenced to six years hard labour. Meanwhile, the police traced the receipt for the camera used to photograph the documents back to Edith. Tommy was with her when they came to arrest Edith. They told her to arrange for someone to look after her son while she went in for questioning. Shaking, she walked Tommy to her brother Wolf's house and left him with Wolf and his wife, before going to the police station, where she was questioned for hours. They wouldn't let Edith rest. They kept asking her question after question, again and again, hounding her for information. What they didn't realize was that, years earlier, Edith had been arrested and interrogated by the secret police in Vienna, after they discovered she had been giving out leaflets trying to recruit communists.

That was in 1933, and compared to four days
in a cell being questioned by Nazi officers, this
interrogation was nothing.

She hadn't broken then, and she didn't break
in London.

Tommy was a little older by the time Edith was
working with a scientist named Engelbert Broda,
helping hand over secrets about the **atomic bomb**
from the Cavendish Laboratory at Cambridge
University. An atomic bomb is a weapon that
has the ability to wipe out entire cities, killing
millions, and the possibility of an enemy creating
one of these was a real fear during the Second
World War. The United States did create one,
dropping an atomic bomb on Hiroshima in Japan,
on 6 August 1945, killing 140,000 people. The US
claimed they did it in order to force the Japanese
government to surrender, ending the war. And
it worked. But Edith believes they also wanted
to send a warning to the Soviet Union about the
strength of the American army.

History has a way of looking back and trying
to make sense of things in a straight line, but
life isn't like that. We must remember why

people make the choices they make, what they are fighting against. Edith knew why she did what she did. She worked for the communists because communism seemed to be the only way of fighting the Nazis. The world was in crisis in the 1930s. Hitler was on the move, and fascism was sweeping through Europe. In communism, Edith and many others (including many British people, in the beginning) believed they had found the solution. This, they thought, was a way to change the world for good.

Edith did have some doubts about what she did, looking back. Particularly when she thought about the Soviet leader, Joseph Stalin – who, it turned out, was not a good man. He killed many of his own people, and put even more in camps. His regime was cruel and paranoid. But in the end, Edith felt she had to separate in her mind the leader and his actions from the ideas that she loved. The ideology that she thought would change the world.

Ideology is a set of beliefs and faiths. Edith's real faith was always communism. And Karl Marx – the founder of Marxist Communism, which Edith followed – said that if things weren't yet well with the world, then we weren't yet at the 'final epoch'. By which he meant it wasn't over yet.

Edith liked to believe that it still wasn't. That there was still time for her ideas to be proven right.

Edith had a friend by the name of Jack Pritchard who created a building in London called the Isokon, where lots of interesting people lived, including artists and spies. He gave safe haven to many refugees from Europe after the war, and offered them jobs at his furniture factory. Jack was a great man, and he once said: 'There are many who want to stir up the status quo and search for a better way to go.'

What he meant was that: in this world, there are people who will stick their necks out to try to change things for the better. They won't always be right. One person's traitor is another person's hero, after all.

But hopefully they will have believed they were doing the right thing, and surely that counts for something.

# TOOLS OF HER TRADE
## ROLLEIFLEX CAMERA

I think it's a shame that Edith's spying sometimes distracts from her great talent as a photographer. Her photos are mainly in black and white, but they show so much of human life, ranging from children playing in the rubble of London after bombs fell during the war, to unemployed Welsh miners marching for fair rights.

Edith used an old-fashioned type of camera called a Rolleiflex. Her first-ever Rolleiflex was given to her by a man called Arnold Deutsch, her Soviet handler. Deutsch, who came from Central Europe, was a little older than Edith, and she was in awe of him. Though he was engaged to someone else (a woman called Josefine who worked with Edith at the nursery in Vienna), he and Edith had a relationship. It was Arnold who told her she should go to train in photography at the Bauhaus.

The camera, Deutsch said, would also be a great tool for spying. And it was. At that time, few people had cameras or knew how to use them. Edith was able to use her Rolleiflex to photograph secret documents like those from the Woolwich Arsenal, which almost led to her being found out as a spy.

Taking photos also gave Edith an excuse for being somewhere she shouldn't. For example, once she was told during a police interrogation that she had been seen on a communist march, and she replied that she was simply there taking photos for a newspaper. Photography was a way of making money, and Edith worked for magazines and even the British government's Ministry of Information and Ministry of Education.

But photography was also a way of making sense of the world. Edith used her talent to show the world as she saw it – to show us the issues she cared about.

## HISTORY DECODED

### THE COLD WAR

The Cold War was a struggle between communist countries in the east, and capitalist countries in the west. The United States and the Soviet Union had fought together as allies during the Second World War. But afterwards, the two superpowers were fighting for influence across the world. The United States and its allies, including the UK, were supporters of democracy and capitalism — which means they supported people's right to vote, to choose a government and to run businesses without interference from that government.

Meanwhile, the Soviet Union — a huge group of countries including Russia, Belarus and Ukraine — was communist. They believed that wealth should be shared among everyone and that no one should be richer than anyone else. For much of the Soviet Union's existence, Joseph Stalin was in charge. He was a dictator who had led the Soviet Union since 1922 and would continue to do so until 1953. His cruel dictatorship led to the deaths of millions of Soviet citizens.

From the mid-1940s until the late 1980s, there was serious tension between east and west, and nuclear war seemed a very real possibility. Then, in 1989, the Berlin Wall in Germany was knocked down.

It had divided the city — and Europe — between east and west for almost three decades, and its collapse marked the beginning of the end for the Soviet Union. In 1991, fifteen new countries emerged, and the Cold War was over.

## HISTORY DECODED

### THE CAMBRIDGE FIVE

The Cambridge Five was a small but infamous group of double agents who met while studying at the University of Cambridge and ended up spying for the Soviet Union. Some say there were more than five of them, but the most famous were Guy Burgess, Donald Maclean, Kim Philby — also known as the Third Man — and Anthony Blunt. The fifth, John Cairncross, was identified with certainty only in 1990.

The Cambridge Five are considered great traitors because they were all well connected, upper-class English gentlemen. Blunt, for instance, was a respected art historian and a third cousin of Queen Elizabeth, the Queen Mother. As a result, these spies had access to powerful people and organizations in Britain and so were able to give away a huge number of important British secrets to the Soviets during the Second World War, and then during the Cold War. This led to the deaths of countless people — and it was very embarrassing for the British government.

# SECRETARY OF THE COMMUNIST PARTY OF GREAT BRITAIN IS MI5 MOLE!

With her dyed blonde hair and glamorous dress, Olga Gray looks every inch a secret agent. But when the Communist Party of Great Britain (CPGB) hired her to work as their secretary, they had no reason to suspect that Olga was really a mole. And that she had been placed there by their enemies – MI5!

Olga Gray was first recruited to the British intelligence services at the age of just 24, by MI5 spymaster Maxwell Knight. When she agreed to go undercover inside the headquarters of the Communist Party of Great Britain, she put her life on the line. For if Russia and its deadly assassins found out what Olga was really up to, she would become enemy number one.

Known to the public only as Miss X, at the time Olga Gray was described by one police detective as 'the bravest girl I ever knew'. Her first mission for MI5 was to become a part of the Communist Party of Great Britain and spy on them, to see if she could find links between the CPGB and Britain's enemy, Soviet Russia. After a year she was taken on by an important person in the CPGB, Percy Glading. Glading had studied at the International Lenin School, in Moscow, which was a training school for Soviet agents, where students were taught about communist politics, and given secret spying skills.

Olga won Glading's trust after being sent by the CPGB on a mission to India. She was then put in charge of running a Soviet safe house in London, which was a secret building owned by the CPGB that could be used to photograph important documents or to host meetings between spies and their handlers. Here she welcomed many important people, including Theodore Maly, a handler of the Austrian recruiter Edith Tudor-Hart and double agent Kim Philby.

When Olga alerted MI5 to top-secret documents being photographed in the flat, MI5 swooped in and arrested Glading, who was sentenced to six years hard labour.

Meanwhile, Olga Gray has been hailed a national hero.

# ZHENG PINGRU

Zheng Pingru was a beautiful socialite, who spent her time attending glamorous parties and gracing the cover of popular women's magazines. Looking at her on those covers, I find it hard to imagine that, at the same time, she was secretly working as a spy for the Republic of China and was gathering intelligence on the Imperial Japanese Army during the war between China and Japan. Harder still is to imagine that at the age of just 22, she would be killed by Shanghai's Security Police.

Zheng was born in Lianxi, Zhejiang Province, National Republic of China, in 1918, and was executed in February 1940, in Shanghai, China. She was half Chinese and half Japanese, and her story is fascinating. Zheng was so young when she spied for

China against the Japanese. Already, she was so sure of herself and what she believed in.

Her father was a follower of Sun Yat-sen, who was the first leader of the Nationalist Party of China, the Kuomintang. He taught at Fudan University in Shanghai in China, and helped inspire his daughter to study at the Shanghai College of Politics and Law. Her mother was from Japan, which meant Zheng spoke fluent Japanese and was able to pretend to be from Japan herself. This was important when she later became a spy for the Kuomintang.

At that time, the Kuomintang were fighting to protect China as a republic (a country where power is held by the people, and run by a government they have voted for), which it had been since the revolution that overthrew the Qing dynasty (the last ruling family in China). They were also having to defend themselves against an invasion by Japan. During this period there was lots of fighting in China between people who wanted different things for their country's future. It is often said that when a country is not united it becomes weak and vulnerable to attack, and in this instance, Japan took advantage.

Zheng was just 13 years old when Japan invaded, in 1931. Her parents took her and her siblings to the anti-Japanese protests that were happening at the time. When the Second World War broke out in 1939, Japan sided with the European fascist leaders Hitler and Mussolini, and China with Britain and its Allies. At this time, Shanghai was run by a brutal group of men. They achieved power using a violent mixture of secret police, assassins and gangsters.

One of the men at the top of this group was Ding Mocun.

In 1940, 22-year-old Zheng Pingru was executed by Shanghai's pro-Japan Security Police after she tried to have Ding Mocun assassinated.

She never saw her beloved Republican government defeated by the Communists, who took power in China in 1949, and remain in power today.

As a child, Zheng wanted to become an actress, like the famous performers she admired, Hu Die and Ruan Lingyu. But her father forbade it. Yet Zheng's work as a secret agent did involve pretending to be someone else entirely, and never giving herself away.

They say truth is stranger than fiction, and this is the final reason why Zheng's story is so fascinating to me. When I hear about the way she tried to lure her enemy to his death, picturing her looking through rows of fur coats with one eye on the assassins waiting in the dark outside, it is like something from a film . . .

Unfortunately in this story, our heroine cannot be saved.

Zheng is being transported towards her execution. She has come to terms with her fate. Her life was short, but it never lacked meaning. She made every moment of her 22 years count.

When she goes to sleep at night, she remembers the moment she led Ding Mocun to what should have been *his* execution. She pictures him standing in the corner of the clothes shop as she trailed her finger along the row of fur coats, pretending to be thinking about which colour and style to choose. From the corner of Zheng's eye, she was watching out for the signal from the assassins who were lurking in the shadows, waiting to take out her enemy.

That was the moment everything changed. And now it is Zheng hurtling towards her death. Although unlike the traitor Ding Mocun, Zheng knows what is coming for her.

Her father was always her inspiration. And her mother. She is proud to have been born half-Japanese, because if her mother hadn't been born and raised in Japan she would never have learned the language and culture, which she appreciates is part of her heritage. She also would have been no use to the Republic of China when it needed her. She believes that this was her fate.

The events of Zheng's childhood and the marches she attended with her parents made a big mark on her life. From a young age, she was in no doubt about what was right and wrong, and that made it easy for her to become a spy for the Kuomintang. Because she spoke perfect Japanese, and because of her family connections on her mother's side, she was able to collect information about the Japanese Army and take it to her commanders. She imagines that her beauty and charm helped, too. Even though she was smart and educated she could, for instance, act the dim playful socialite, while all along working on the plot to assassinate Ding Mocun.

Even now, she can hardly say his name. The name of an agent of the Kuomintang, and head of security for the Republic of China, who betrayed her so deeply by working with the Japanese.

Her job should have been easy. Zheng could make people believe she was who they wanted her to be. And she already knew Butcher Ding (as she called Ding Mocun) – he had been the principal of her secondary school. She was tasked with making him fall in love with her and then luring him into a trap. And it so nearly worked. In March 1939, she started to bump into Ding out and about, pretending the meetings were a coincidence. Soon she succeeded in making him her boyfriend.

The plan was to lure Butcher Ding to a quiet spot and have him killed. But the first night she attempted to do this, while the assassins waited in place at her home, Ding must have grown suspicious. He refused to come with her, and, having failed, Zheng was forced to return home alone.

The second attempt is the reason why she is now hurtling down the Zhongshan Road in Western Shanghai, on the way to her death.

That winter, on 21 December 1939, Ding and Zheng went for dinner with friends. All evening she laughed and played along, acting the good girlfriend. On their way back, Zheng asked him if they might stop off at the Siberia Fur Company on

Shanghai's famous shopping street, Nanjing Road. Making it clear to Ding how much she valued his taste and opinion, she asked him to help her choose a new fur coat, leading him inside the shop. Meanwhile, two Kuomintang assassins took their places outside the doors, ready for their exit.

But Ding seemed to have a sixth sense for danger. While Zheng scanned the coats, he became anxious, as if he knew what was coming. Looking about, he spotted the men waiting outside and fled on foot to his car, his driver speeding him away to safety.

Of course, after that, he knew Zheng was a spy. When he next asked to meet her, at the headquarters of the Chinese secret police, she arrived with a pistol hidden in her handbag, ready to do the job herself. But before she could enter the address at 76 Jessfield Road, Shanghai, she was arrested by the head of the secret police and held there. That was two months ago.

During these past weeks, Zheng has suffered. At first, they tried to make her join their side – to turn her into a double agent. The head of the secret police, Wang Jingwei, even brought in his wife, who attempted to persuade Zheng to join her husband's evil regime and spy against China, for the Japanese. But of course Zheng wouldn't. And when she refused, they held her as a **hostage**, trying to use her to get to her father. She's proud that he also refused their invitation to join them.

One day, she will be remembered as a martyr – one who died for a cause she believed in. She is confident of this. Perhaps one day her story will even inspire a film, and she will be played by a great actress like the ones she used to watch.

Whatever happens now, her death will have meaning.

But she is sorry for what this will do to her father and mother. She is grateful to both of them for teaching her right from wrong, from an early age. They gave her the strength to make the right choice. Even if she paid for that with her life.

# TOOLS OF HER TRADE
## IMPERSONATION

From a young age, Zheng Pingru wanted to be an actress, admiring stars such as Hu Die and Ruan Lingyu. Her father disapproved of this ambition and she ended up going to university instead, but she never lost her passion for impersonation. It was this ability to present herself as someone she was not that enabled her to pose as Japanese and become the spy that she was.

# SUE DOBSON: THE SPY SOUTH AFRICA NEVER CAUGHT

'Very ordinary'. These are the words used by Sue Dobson to describe herself. Anyone else might say that Dobson's secret life as a spy, fighting racism during Apartheid in South Africa, was anything but.

Apartheid means 'apartness' in Afrikaans, a language spoken in South Africa and other countries. It was the name for a set of laws introduced by the National Party government in South Africa, from 1948. These laws kept white people apart from other people, and treated anyone who was not white (which was most people in South Africa at the time) as second-class citizens with fewer rights and powers in all aspects of everyday life, from jobs to housing.

Sue Dobson was a white middle-class woman in her twenties who secretly joined the African National Congress (ANC), a group that wanted to end Apartheid. When she joined, Sue was set the task of getting as close to the government as she could, to discover information that would help the ANC. And she succeeded in getting very close indeed. Speaking to the *Observer* newspaper, she said: 'It's because I'm ordinary that I was able to do the work that I did, because I wasn't suspected ... My ordinariness has been my strength, strangely.'

Whether her ordinariness or her courage was her superpower is open to debate. But what is definitely true is that she successfully got through the first rounds of security clearance (the official checks into a person to make sure they can be trusted) and managed to gain access to important people in the government.

Pretending to be a supporter of the National Party, Sue first worked as a journalist for a newspaper called the *Citizen*, which supported the government. Then she worked for the information bureau, which holds government records. But all along, she was also working as a spy for the ANC, passing them secret documents and useful information.

At the time, the Soviet Union was helping to train members of the ANC. They were doing this because the ANC were trying to overthrow the government as part of ending Apartheid, and the Soviet Union wanted to help get rid of the existing government and replace it with a socialist one.

Dobson and her husband (also a member of the ANC) had been trained by the Soviets in intelligence work. They used radios to secretly communicate, carried out dead-letter drops, used invisible ink, and even created explosives. Most dangerous of all, Dobson had started a relationship with a police officer in order to find out information from the police that she could pass on to the ANC.

If she had been caught as a spy for the African National Congress, Dobson would have been charged with treason and put in prison (where she would have faced torture) for fifteen years.

She very nearly was.

In 1989, while Dobson was working for the government's information bureau, she was considered for a promotion to work in the office of the president, F. W. de Klerk. Again, she had to go through security checks. But, this time, it was discovered that Dobson's sister-in-law was a member of the ANC and her cover was blown. She was 'burned'.

One dark night, and with the help of the Soviets, Sue Dobson fled South Africa to nearby Botswana by car. In Botswana, she was put on a flight to London, where she was finally safe.

Afterwards, Dobson faced death threats and, back in South Africa, the government seized all her possessions. She was added to a list of people the government wanted dead, and spent many years checking her post for letter bombs (explosives that arrive hidden in the post, disguised as regular parcels).

Her enemies took everything from Sue Dobson that they could, but they never took her freedom.

# SARASWATHI
# RAJAMANI

'When I grow up, I'm going to shoot an Englishman.'
These were the words of the girl who would become
known as India's youngest spy, spoken to Mahatma
Gandhi when she was just ten years old.

This was in 1937, and there had already been conflict
in India for decades. As we know from Noor Inayat
Khan's story (see page 128), for nearly 90 years Britain
had ruled India, having controlled it since 1858.

And we know that many in India wanted an end
to British rule, believing that its people should be
allowed to run the country themselves. Not everyone
had the same idea as to how to make this happen,
though. Mahatma Gandhi, you'll remember, believed

in the power of pacifism – taking action but not being violent.

But there were those who wanted to fight. And this is what Saraswathi Rajamani decided she wanted to do, at a very young age.

In a tale that is worthy of **Bollywood**, Saraswathi Rajamani joined forces with another female volunteer, named Durga, on a mission to spy on British soldiers. This means that as the Second World War raged, from 1939 to 1945, Rajamani and Noor Inayat Khan would be fighting on opposite sides, though their paths never crossed.

Rajamani was born on 11 January 1927 in Myanmar (a country that was at the time called Burma), and died on 13 January 2018, in Peters Colony in Chennai, India. Her family was one of the richest in Rangoon, the part of Myanmar where they lived. Like a number of others in the area they had left India to escape persecution by the British.

The story of Saraswathi and Gandhi in 1937 is worth telling. Gandhi was visiting former citizens of British India, to try and encourage them to join his non-violent plan for India to be free from British rule. During his visit, one of the children, a 10-year-old girl named Rajamani, went missing. When Gandhi went into the garden to look for her, he found her holding a toy gun. Rajamani told him that she was practising shooting Englishmen because that's what you did with thieves. And this was what the British were in India: thieves of her homeland.

'Mahatma' is a name given to someone both loved and respected, and it is true that Gandhi's message of winning independence peacefully made an impression on the child. But she, like many others, didn't believe peaceful action would be enough.

In 1944, at the age of 16, Rajamani heard Netaji Subhas Chandra Bose speak about how he intended to fight the British, to take back India by force.

She was so inspired by him, she took notes on his speech.

Her father, who owned a gold mine, had already given a lot of money to Bose's organization, and the teenage Rajamani tried to donate all of her own money and jewellery too. Bose refused to accept it, given her age. Instead, he got her to join the fight – which seems pretty extraordinary to me! Perhaps he understood straight away that her real value was in her commitment to freedom.

It was Bose who gave Rajamani the name 'Saraswathi', meaning wisdom, and signed her up to the Indian National Army (INA), which fought against the British in the Second World War, under the command of Japan. Here she began nursing wounded soldiers, before becoming an armed fighter and spy.

As we have already seen, during the Second World War Japan joined the Axis forces alongside Germany and Italy. And so though the story of Bose made him a hero among many Indians at the time, it soon turned sour following his wartime alliances with Nazi Germany and Imperial Japan. After the war, with Bose's army falling apart, Rajamani's family returned to India. Rajamani lived until the age of 91.

Today, it is acknowledged that Rajamani's work contributed to Indian Independence. She was a freedom fighter from childhood, and considered herself such until the very end.

S araswathi is growing old. She will be 91 soon. But she still thinks of herself as the spirited child she was all those years ago: the youngest spy in the Indian National Army. And she still has her medals and the scar from the bullet in her leg to prove it . . .

She thinks back to her first mission. How she and her friend Durga cut their hair and disguised themselves as errand boys, fetching tea or delivering messages in order to spy on British military camps and British officers' homes. It is unbelievable to Saraswathi, looking back now, that they got away with their undercover disguise for so long. Perhaps those men just couldn't have imagined that they were being tricked by girls!

Her story might have begun with that visit from the Mahatma. But really it was the moment she heard Netaji Subhas Chandra Bose speak that she knew what she had to do. It was all very well *wanting* freedom, but without *action*, she thought, it would be impossible.

If she wanted independence for India, she believed she had to take it. It was Bose's message which stayed with Saraswathi: 'Give me blood and I shall give you freedom.'

Those were the words that rang through her ears as Saraswathi and Durga entered the British officers' private rooms – part of the British military base in Kolkata, in the east of India. She will never forget that moment. When that officer gave her a single look, before turning his back. Could they really have got away with it, she wondered? Until that point, Saraswathi wouldn't have believed that the soldiers might ever turn away long enough for her and Durga to rummage through their belongings. But they did! She was almost too stunned to move. Then, just like that, she came to her senses again and set to work.

That first time, Saraswathi's hands prickled with sweat as they rifled through the British files, trying to find the information they needed. But it became more natural as the days and weeks went on. They started to find important bits and pieces, which they slipped inside their clothes, to pass back to their bosses at the Indian National Army. They got plenty that was useful. But then they found that single piece of paper – the paper showing the British plan to assassinate Saraswathi's leader and hero, Bose. And Saraswathi knew that this had been her life's mission. Together, Saraswathi and Durga were able to warn Bose and save his life.

And they didn't stop there. The pair continued spying on those grown men right up until the moment they caught Durga, and put her in prison! Of course, Saraswathi wasn't going to leave her best friend there. It is perhaps her proudest moment, breaking Durga out of that prison.

Even now, more than seven decades later, she still thinks of it.

Her plan was simple. She knew that British troops brought in local girls; dancers who would perform for the troops when they got bored and wanted entertaining.

One evening, Saraswathi dressed as a dancer and arrived unannounced at the gates of the prison where Durga was being held. She told the British troops that she had been invited by another officer, and batted her eyelids as they let her in. Once she was inside, she offered to fetch the guards on duty a cup of chai. She hardly dared risk looking behind her as she tipped the crushed-up sleeping pill (the one she'd carried inside her top) into the cups.

Willing her hands not to shake, Saraswathi handed the drinks to the men without making eye contact. For a moment, as they sipped, she worried they would taste the medicine and she would be done for. But they didn't notice a thing. In only a few minutes they fell asleep, and Saraswathi was able to slip the key from one of their pockets and find Durga's cell. Her hands did finally shake as the key rattled in the lock; and then, suddenly, the padlock was open and the two friends were reunited! It was then that Saraswathi realized they were only part way through the plan. Durga was out of her prison cell, but they weren't yet free.

The prison was surrounded by guards, and by the time Durga was free another soldier had returned and found the sleeping prison officers. He immediately guessed what had happened.

Saraswathi remembers how they clutched each other's hands as they ran. And the sound of the soldiers' feet as they ran after them, shooting their guns. More than the feeling of the bullet as it hit her leg, Saraswathi remembers Durga's hand in hers, and how she thought that, together, they were stronger and faster than the soldiers.

She was right. Even after they shot Saraswathi, the pair were quicker-witted than the soldiers. They climbed up a tree and stayed there for hours, until the British called off their search and they were able to climb down and escape to freedom.

Freedom, when it came, came at a price. The road following Indian independence was long and bloody. Nevertheless, Saraswathi is proud to have played her part.

But in these final weeks of her life, Saraswathi thinks of her and Durga, running, hand in hand. She thinks of them, high up in those branches, awaiting the moment they could return to the land that was rightly theirs.

# TOOLS OF HER TRADE
## CONFIDENCE

From a young age, Saraswathi Rajamani had real confidence in her beliefs, and in her own ability to make a difference. She knew who she was and how she wanted to change the world. This strength of character meant Saraswathi was able to convince others, like Bose, that she was someone who could be relied on. It also enabled her to pretend to be someone else (like a tea-boy) and deceive her enemies.

*8 JULY 1982*

# WE CELEBRATE THE LIFE OF A FEARLESS OSS FIELD AGENT!

For many reasons, the American spy Virginia Hall was celebrated as one of the most incredible field agents in the British Special Operations Executive. After studying at three separate American universities, she travelled around Europe, with a dream of joining the Foreign Service, working for the United States abroad.

This was a dream that seemed likely to be cut short when, in Turkey, Hall was involved in a serious hunting accident.

After the accident, Hall contracted gangrene – a serious condition, where parts of the body begin to die – and she herself nearly died as a result of the infection. She lost one of her legs and was told she would only ever be able to have a job at a desk, and could never become an agent in the field, spying on enemy soldiers and sabotaging equipment – something she longed to do.

But she was not put off.

At the beginning of the Second World War, she served as an ambulance driver in France. When France was invaded by Nazi Germany, she made her way to Spain and met a British intelligence officer. She told him she intended to go to England, and he suggested he call a friend of his, who worked for the newly created SOE. She was accepted into SOE, and went through rigorous training before becoming the first female spy to live behind enemy lines in France during the war. Here, her work involved recruiting other spies and organizing Resistance fighters against the Nazis, who were occupying the country at the time. She also ran safe houses, where spies could hide from their enemies and report back to London on the German army, using **Morse code**.

Cruel and aggressive, the Nazis behaved terribly in occupied France. As Hall said: 'I've never seen so much hatred.'

During her first 13 months as a spy in the country, she sometimes disguised herself as a farmer and pretended to herd cows while undergoing secret missions at drop zones. These drop zones were places where Allied planes might drop supplies, or other agents, by parachute. Or they could be places where it might be possible to ambush German soldiers.

She did all of this – and more – with an artificial limb, staying one step ahead of the Gestapo (German secret police) for more than a year until it became clear the Germans were aware that there was a spy in their midst.

Knowing her time was up, Hall fled before being caught, and returned to the United States where she joined the Office of Strategic Services (OSS), which was the organization that would later become America's infamous Central Intelligence Agency (the CIA). A year before the war ended, in 1944, she returned to France to once again work for the Resistance.

After the war ended in 1945, Hall was awarded the Distinguished Service Cross, and became the only American woman in history to have been given this honour.

# ZANDRA FLEMISTER

I wanted to end this book with the inspiring story of Zandra Flemister, who stood up against both the racism and the sexism she faced while serving her country.

Zandra was the first African American woman to have been hired by the US Secret Service. When she died in 2023, at the age of 71, she was remembered by the woman now in charge of the Secret Service, Kimberly Cheatle, as a hero and trailblazer, who 'inspired a future generation of agents'.

Zandra spent years fighting against discrimination in the organization for which she worked as a spy. When she joined the Secret Service in 1974, it had been just three years since it had hired its first female member, and women were often treated unfairly, with fewer opportunities given to them. But Zandra also faced discrimination from people because of the colour of her skin – which led to her taking the Secret Service to court.

Tragically, when Zandra was in her fifties, she began to suffer from Alzheimer's, an illness that slowly destroys memory and thinking skills, and makes daily tasks much more difficult. This prevented her from seeing the legal case against the Secret Service through to the end. Her condition was so bad that she had to take early retirement at the age of 59.

But she will be remembered as a brilliant and brave agent, and **activist**.

Zandra was born in Frankfurt, Germany, in 1951 to American parents. She was raised in the United States and studied political science at Northeastern University in Boston, Massachusetts.

She believed, like her parents before her, that she was born to serve her country. Her father was a US Army sergeant and her mother worked for the government as a microfilm technician, which meant she processed and scanned documents. Because of her father's job, the family moved around a lot when Zandra was young, which was good training for her future career.

After her parents separated, when Zandra was just five years old, she and her mother moved to Connecticut, to a quaint, picture-perfect spot on the East Coast of America, with white clapboard houses and big trees. It was her mother who taught her to fight for what she believed in.

Zandra had a pretty uneventful childhood, learning to play the piano and taking ballet classes. But, at weekends, her mother would take her on **civil rights demonstrations**, demanding the same rights for Black people as there were for white people. It was during the 1963 March on Washington, where 250,000 people gathered to call for an end to racism and racial discrimination, that the twelve-year-old Zandra saw that the fight for equality was worthwhile. Martin Luther King's 'I Have a Dream' speech would have been ringing in her ears.

After graduating from college in Massachusetts, not far from where she grew up, Zandra met a Secret Service agent who said she should apply to work as a special agent. She did, and was accepted, in 1974.

So it was at the age of 23 that Zandra became the first African American woman to serve as a United States special agent, working for the Secret Service, whose role is to protect American politicians and their families.

During her time in the organization, Zandra was put in charge of protecting mainly women, including the daughters of the president (this was the reason women were first allowed into the Secret Service). But Zandra was more than capable of keeping anyone safe and of doing any job a man could.

Yet just four years after signing up, Zandra resigned from her job because of the racism she faced. Racism she went on to describe in detail, in court, years later.

When she joined the service, Zandra believed she could work her way up through the ranks. It was just a matter of time, and being the best agent she could be. But no matter how hard she worked, or how good she was at her job, her requests for promotion or transfer to better jobs were denied time and again. People she worked with were constantly questioning the work she had done, and whether she had the skills needed to do it. There was racist language used against her by people in the Secret Service, and she was told by her employers that she would need to get rid of her Afro-style hair if she wanted a promotion. One agent even mistook her for a prisoner while they were both on duty, because of their prejudice against the colour of her skin.

In 1978, Zandra left the Secret Service, taking a job in the Foreign Service instead. She was always unflappable in a crisis, and in her new role she got the career she deserved, making it into the upper ranks of the organization and working all over the world.

Once she got to where she wanted to be, Zandra was able to fight for what she hadn't been given, and for what she wanted the next generation to have.

In the year 2000, Zandra became one of more than a hundred Black agents who took the Secret Service to court. The lawsuit they filed accused the agency of racial discrimination, stating that she and others had not been allowed to have successful careers in the Secret Service because of their race.

Very sadly, because of her ill health, Zandra was not able to see the legal case against the Secret Service through to the end.

In February 2023, Zandra died. But her bravery and her sense of justice will live on.

# GREAT FICTIONAL
# KID SPIES

## *ROSIE RAJA: CHURCHILL'S SPY* BY SUFIYA AHMED

A brilliant new agent, Rosie Raja is the determined
Muslim heroine of this historical adventure in which
she discovers her father isn't who she thought. Through
the course of the book, Rosie becomes involved in a
struggle against the Nazis in occupied France.

## THE *HIS DARK MATERIALS* SERIES BY
## PHILIP PULLMAN

Not officially a spy novel, but with a sharp eye for rooting
out villains and a strong radar for adventure, I would
wager that Lyra Belacqua, the heroine of the trilogy
*His Dark Materials*, is as good a spy as they come.

### THE MINISTRY OF UNLADYLIKE ACTIVITY BY ROBIN STEVENS

The younger sister of Hazel Wong (a character in Robin Stevens's popular *Murder Most Unladylike* series) takes her turn going undercover and becomes a ten-year-old secret agent during the Second World War.

### HARRIET THE SPY BY LOUISE FITZHUGH

Published in 1964, this classic tale is about Harriet M. Welsch, an eleven-year-old aspiring writer who, as practise for her future career as a secret agent, observes and makes notes about her neighbours and classmates. But there are dramatic consequences when she loses the notebook and it is found by some of those featured in its pages!

### RUBY REDFORT SERIES BY LAUREN CHILD

Ruby Redfort is a girl with an extraordinary memory that helps her to solve difficult, daring mysteries that unfold over the course of this popular series by the author of those other hellraisers, Charlie and Lola.

## TAYLOR & ROSE SECRET AGENTS SERIES BY KATHERINE WOODFINE

Set in the early twentieth century, Miss Sophie Taylor and Miss Lilian Rose are recruited by a spy agency as secret agents who travel around the world. From Russia to New York, they go undercover to solve mysteries.

# GLOSSARY

**Activist:** A person who wants laws or attitudes to change and is prepared to do something about it.

**Atomic bomb:** A powerful, destructive weapon. When a plutonium or uranium atom is split, it triggers a massive chain reaction, releasing huge amounts of energy as a violent explosion.

**Bedouin:** People who live in the deserts of the Middle East and North Africa, moving from place to place.

**Blitz:** The destructive and relentless bombing campaign that Nazi Germany unleashed on British cities from September 1940 to May 1941. 'Blitz' comes from the German word 'Blitzkrieg', which means 'lightning war'.

**Bollywood:** The Indian film industry, famous for its imaginative plots and wildly exciting song and dance routines. The word is a mixture of Bombay (the old name for the Indian city of Mumbai) and 'Hollywood' – the home of the USA film industry.

**Civil rights:** Rights that guarantee everyone is equal under law, regardless of race, religion or other characteristics. Civil rights ensure everyone has the same opportunities in life, and include the right to vote, the right to a fair trial and the right to education.

**Civil rights demonstrations:** When crowds of people gather to campaign for rights that guarantee equality..

**Concentration camp:** A place where people are imprisoned without trial and live in appalling conditions. During the Second World War, the Nazis killed a horrifyingly large number of people in over a thousand concentration camps. Anyone the Nazis decided did not fit their idea of a so-called 'pure' race was in danger. Millions of Jewish, Romani, Black, Slavic, disabled and gay people were killed. Those with different political or religious views also died.

**Conscientious objector:** Someone who refuses to fight in a war because of their beliefs.

**Courier:** In the world of spying, a courier is someone who carries top-secret information from one place to another.

**D-Day:** The name for the day when a military operation begins. D-Day now usually refers to 6 June 1944 during the Second World War, when Operation Overlord began. This was the codename for the Allied invasion of north-west Europe. Thousands of ships and troops landed on five Normandy beaches to begin a campaign to overthrow the Nazis.

**Diplomat:** A person who represents a country's government in another country. For example, a British diplomat might work in Singapore, representing the British government in that country.

**Discrimination:** When someone is treated unfairly because of their race, sex or age.

**Firing squad:** A group of armed soldiers who execute someone. Soldiers are not told who has live ammunition and which guns contain blanks. So, as everyone fires at exactly the same time, no one knows who killed the victim.

**Foreign Service:** Government officials who are responsible for looking after a country's businesses and citizens overseas.

**French Resistance:** The people who secretly worked together to fight against the Nazis after they invaded France in the Second World War.

**Government:** An organization with the power and authority to make rules and govern a country and its people.

**Hard labour:** When prisoners are forced to do physically hard work as part of their prison sentence.

**Hostage:** Someone who is held captive until others agree a deal or pay ransom money to set them free.

**Imperialist rule:** When a country takes over other countries and controls them.

**Kaiser Wilhelm II:** The last German emperor (ruler of Germany) and king of Prussia. At the end of the First World War, he was forced to give up his throne.

**Maginot Line:** A series of defences that France had built up along its border with Germany during the 1930s, designed to prevent an invasion. At the start of the Second World War, in May 1940, Nazi Germany found a way to bypass this line and invade France.

**Microfilm:** Photographic film that shows tiny copies of documents, books or newspapers.

**Middle class:** People who have a good standard of education and well-paid jobs are known as 'middle class'. They earn more than the poorest people in society, but not as much as those who are very wealthy.

**Military court:** A court of law especially for those in the armed forces.

**Military line:** The very edge of an area controlled by soldiers.

**Morse code:** A code in which the letters of the alphabet are represented by combinations of dots and dashes.

**Mutiny:** When soldiers or sailors rebel against those in charge.

**Ottoman Empire:** Founded in 1299 by Turkish tribes, the Ottoman Empire was once a world superpower, with control of south-east Europe, West Asia and North Africa. But when it entered the First World War on the side of the Central Powers – and was then defeated – the empire was in serious decline. By 1922, it was all over. After the war, the Ottoman Empire was split into countries that would be administered by Allied nations.

**Pension:** A certain amount of money given to someone to live on once they have reached a particular age, normally in their later years.

**Prohibition:** When something is forbidden. In the 1920s and 1930s in the USA, Prohibition was the law that made it illegal to produce or sell alcohol.

**Propaganda:** Misleading information designed to make people think in a certain way or believe one side of an argument. Propaganda does not give a balanced view.

**Quaker:** A member of a Christian movement. Quakers believe in living very simple lives.

**Regime:** A strict government and the way it operates. In Italy during the 1920s and 1930s, Mussolini's regime was violent and harsh.

**Saboteur:** Someone involved in sabotage. Sabotage is when a person or organization deliberately destroys or damages something, or stops an event from happening. It often occurs during a war, when one side will sabotage another to gain an advantage.

**Scapegoat:** A person who is blamed for someone else's mistakes.

**Schizophrenia:** A serious mental health condition that affects the way someone feels and behaves. Sufferers may see things that are not really there.

**Scholar:** Someone who is an expert in a particular area or subject.

**Secret police:** A police force that works in secret to find and punish its government's enemies.

**Seduction:** Making someone else feel that they are in love.

**Smugglers:** People who secretly and illegally move goods such as drugs, guns or money in or out of a country.

**Solitary confinement:** When a prisoner is kept in a cell on their own, often for long periods of time.

**Women's Auxiliary Air Force:** A women's air force, formed during the Second World War to assist the existing Royal Air Force.

# ACKNOWLEDGEMENTS

This book wouldn't have been possible if it weren't for the research material made available by journalists, biographers, historians and archivists – too many to name – who, through their hard work, have made it possible for writers like me to dig into the histories of people whose stories might otherwise have died with them. Thank you.

The stories in this book are, by their nature, complex. In order to present them in a way that does justice to these complexities, in a sensitive manner, I have relied on the expertise and guidance of a number of early readers. For this, I would like to thank: Alia Bano, Shrabani Basu, Victoria Cho, Michell Chresfield, Erin Forbes, Helen Gould, Justin Ho, Georgina Kamskia, Marisa McGlinchey and Anwesha Roy.

Speaking of early readers, biggest thanks of all to my most critical and enthusiastic editor, my youngest son, Xander. With the occasional input of his older siblings, Jesse and Rosa, he helped bring these tales to life in a way that will hopefully appeal to readers young and old.

Huge thanks to my truly excellent actual editor, Tom Rawlinson, for thinking of me for this fantastic project, and then allowing me such creative freedom; to Kat Goodloe for her fabulous illustrations; and to the crack team at Puffin, including Sarah Connelly, Caroline Curtis, Debs Warner, Hollie Cayzer, Jess Mackay, Alice Todd, Rianna Johnson, Sarah Doyle and Lauren Floodgate, who worked on this book.

Finally, to the women who fought for what they believed: I salute you.

# ABOUT THE AUTHOR

Charlotte Philby is a critically acclaimed author of six novels. As a journalist, she worked for eight years as a newspaper reporter, editor and columnist at the *Independent*, where she was shortlisted for the Cudlipp Prize for investigative reporting. She is a former contributing editor and features writer at *Marie Claire*, and has written for publications including *The Sunday Times, New Statesman* and *Financial Times*. With the support of the BFI, she is currently adapting for film her novel *Edith and Kim*, which re-imagines the lives of her grandfather, the double-agent Kim Philby, and Edith Tudor-Hart, who recruited him to the Soviet cause. Charlotte has three children and lives in Bristol.

**EDITH CAVELL**

**EDITH TUDOR-HART**

**JOSEPHINE BAKER**

**KRYSTYNA SKARBEK**

**SARASWATHI
RAJAMANI**

**ZANDRA FLEMISTER**

**ELIZABETH SMITH-FRIEDMAN**

**HARRIET TUBMAN**

**MATA HARI**

**NOOR INAYAT KHAN**

**ZHENG PINGRU**